FORMS OF WRITING

Workbook

Marian E. Kowler
Diane Ewen
Kay L. Stewart

Prentice-Hall Canada Inc.,
Scarborough, Ontario

Canadian Cataloguing in Publication Data

Stewart, Kay. L. (Kay Lanette), 1942-
Forms of writing workbook
Supplement to: Forms of writing.
ISBN 0-13-327354-7

1. English language - Rhetoric - Problems, exercises, etc. 2. Business writing - Problems, exercises, etc. I. Kowler, Marian, 1945- . II. Ewen, Diane. III. Title.

PE1408.F673 1990   808'.042   C90-095464-7

Prentice-Hall, Inc., Englewood Cliffs, New Jersey
Prentice-Hall International, Inc., London
Prentice-Hall of Australia, Pty., Ltd., Sydney
Prentice-Hall of India Pvt., Ltd., New Delhi
Prentice-Hall of Japan, Inc., Tokyo
Prentice-Hall of Southeast Asia (Pte.) Ltd., Singapore
Editora Prentice-Hall do Brasil Ltda., Rio de Janeiro
Prentice-Hall Hispanoamericana, S.A., Mexico

ISBN 0-13-327354-7

Copy Editor: Jocelyn Smyth
Production Editor: Doris Wolf
Production Coordinator: Lisa Kreuch
Cover Design: Deborah-Anne Bailey

1 2 3 4 5 AP 95 94 93 92 91

Printed and bound in Canada by The Alger Press Limited

Contents

━━━━━━━━━━━━━━━━━━━━━━━━━━ PART 2 ━━━━━

Part 2: Practice With Sentence Structure, Grammar, and Punctuation   69

9. Verbs

10. Pronouns

11. Adjectives and Adverbs   171

12. Punctuation and Mechanics   179

Preface

This workbook is designed to accompany *Forms of Writing: A Brief Guide and Handbook*. We have divided the workbook into two main sections. "Practice with Writing," as its name suggests, gives you more practice with the methods and forms of writing covered in parts 2, 3, and 4 of the text. "Practice with Sentence Structure, Grammar, and Punctuation" gives you more practice with the material covered in Part 5, the handbook section of the text.

"Practice with Writing" has seven main parts. Like the text, it begins with "The Writing Process" and includes more exercises on defining your purpose and specific goal. You will also find more information and exercises on making reader profiles. Parts 2 and 3 of the workbook cover paragraphs, Parts 4 and 5 cover essays, and Parts 6 and 7 cover business letters and reports. Each part contains writing exercises based on the three main purposes for writing: to explain, to share personal experience, and to persuade. In these exercises you will find suggestions for preparing, drafting, and revising each piece of writing. If you want more information on how to develop a particular piece, refer to the appropriate section of the text given in brackets at the beginning of the exercise.

You can get more help on especially troublesome points of grammar, sentence structure, punctuation, and dictionary skills in the second section of the workbook. The handbook in the text covers most of this material, but sometimes working through another set of exercises can make a big difference.

While the name "workbook" does not suggest much fun, we hope that you will enjoy improving your skills and find the material here useful.

PART 1

PRACTICE WITH
WRITING

1

The Writing Process

Defining Your Purpose and Specific Goal

It might seem to you that when you are faced with any piece of writing—a letter, a report, an essay—your purpose is to get the job done. Speedy completion, however, is only one purpose. Your more important purpose is to communicate what you are saying well enough to get your message across to your reader. In this context, purpose has a special meaning. We will use the term *purpose* to refer to the three broad approaches you can take to any subject: to explain, to share personal experience, and to persuade.

[*Forms of Writing,* Part 1: 1a-e]

Let's say you are writing an essay on multiculturalism in Canada. What is your purpose? Do you want to explain the concept of multiculturalism? to share an experience that showed you the importance of respecting the customs of a particular ethnic group? to persuade others that the varied nature of Canadian society has enriched our country? Each of these approaches to the subject of multiculturalism represents one of the three main purposes in writing.

When you know which of these purposes is most appropriate for a particular writing situation, you can work out a more specific goal by focusing on one aspect of your subject. You could write an expository essay providing examples that explain multiculturalism in the context of elementary school language programs. Or you could write a personal essay explaining how your attitudes towards a particular ethnic group have changed. Or you could argue that Canadian television needs to promote the concept of multiculturalism more actively.

Let's take a closer look at this movement from a broad purpose to a more specific goal in expository, personal, and persuasive writing.

3

Writing to Explain

In **expository writing**, you write to inform your readers. You might explain how to do something, how something works, or what something means. When you explain, your emphasis is on your subject, as this diagram suggests.

DIAGRAM A

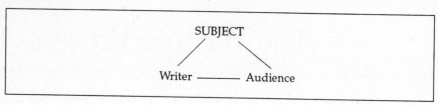

Once you have decided that your broad purpose for a particular piece of writing is to explain, you need to define your specific goal. You can do so by completing one of the following sentences:

My goal is to explain **what** _____.
My goal is to explain **how** _____.
My goal is to explain **why** _____.

Here are examples of specific goals for expository essays or reports on three different subjects.

SUBJECT 1   interest rates
GOAL   to explain the effect of high interest rates on consumer borrowing

SUBJECT 2   oil change
GOAL   to explain how to change the oil in a car

SUBJECT 3   gambling
GOAL   to explain why some people are addicted to gambling

Exercise 1

State a specific goal for a short expository essay on **three** of the following subjects:

1. used cars
2. VCR's
3. dogs
4. a first aid course
5. exercises to avoid

Writing to Share Personal Experience

In **personal writing**, your main purpose is to share your experiences, feelings, or impressions of life. Because your material is so much a part of you, the emphasis in personal writing is on you, the writer.

DIAGRAM B

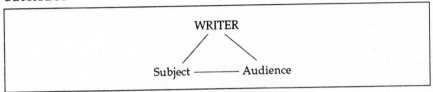

Personal writing can be **narrative**, **descriptive**, or **reflective**. Narrative writing tells a story. Descriptive writing presents your impressions of how something looks, sounds, tastes, smells, or moves. Reflective writing presents your thoughts and feelings on a topic. To define a more specific goal for a piece of personal writing, you would complete one of the following sentences:

NARRATION: My goal is to tell what happened when ————.
DESCRIPTION: My goal is to describe my impressions of ————.
REFLECTION: My goal is to share my reflections about ————.

Here are some examples of specific goals for personal essays on three different subjects.

SUBJECT   an embarrassing experience
GOAL   to tell what happened the day I lost my case in Small
              Claims court

SUBJECT   coming home
GOAL   to describe the changes in my old neighbourhood over
              the past five years

SUBJECT   friendship
GOAL   to share my reflections on the importance of loyalty
              between friends

Exercise 2

State a specific goal for a short personal essay on **three** of the following subjects. Try to make one goal narrative, another descriptive, and another reflective.

1. getting lost
2. seeing _____ for the first time
3. owning my first _____
4. breaking up
5. working for a living

Writing to Persuade

In **persuasive writing,** you want to convince your readers to share your beliefs about your subject. Your focus is on your readers because you will be persuasive only if you choose arguments that appeal to them.

DIAGRAM C

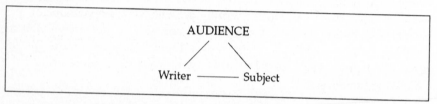

Before beginning a piece of persuasive writing, you can define a more specific goal by completing one of these sentences:

My goal is to convince my readers that _____.
My goal is convince my readers to _____.

Here are specific goals for two pieces of persuasive writing:

SUBJECT   volunteer work
GOAL   to convince my readers that volunteer work can be
            rewarding for the volunteer
SUBJECT   applying for a job
GOAL   to convince my reader to give me an interview for the job
            I'm applying for

Exercise 3

State a specific goal for a short persuasive essay on **three** of the following subjects:

1. a new statutory holiday
2. sex education in elementary schools
3. the use of animals in laboratory experiments
4. voluntary euthanasia for the terminally ill
5. increasing the taxes on cigarettes

Review Exercise: Broad Purposes and Specific Goals

In the sample below, specific goals have been defined for an expository, a personal, and a persuasive essay on the subject of garbage recycling.

1. SUBJECT garbage recycling
   PURPOSE explanation
   GOAL to explain how garbage recycling programs work

2. SUBJECT garbage recycling
   PURPOSE to share my experience
   GOAL to tell what happened when I became obsessed with recycling

3. SUBJECT garbage recycling
   PURPOSE persuasion
   GOAL to convince my readers to recycle their garbage

Using this example as a model, write a specific goal for an expository, a personal, and a persuasive essay on **one** of the following:

1. dating
2. keeping pets in an apartment complex
3. independence
4. exams
5. dieting

Making Reader Profiles

[*Forms of Writing,* Part 1: 1f]

When you are speaking, you often know your listener personally, so it's relatively easy to adjust both what you say and how you say it to suit your listener. If you were talking about your vacation plans with your boss, for example, you would probably focus on factual information—dates, places, travel arrangements—and your language would be fairly formal. If you were discussing these same plans with a friend, you would probably focus more on what you hoped to do and your language would be more informal.

When you write, you're less likely to know your reader personally, so you might wonder how you can meet the needs of this person. The answer is that you can adapt the skills you've developed in speaking to different listeners to writing for different readers. To decide what information to present and how to present it, imagine what a person in the position of your reader—an instructor, a claims adjuster, a prospective employer—would want to know. Here are the basic questions to ask:

1. Who is my reader?
2. What would a person in this position need and want to know?

7

3. What is my position—that of a co-worker, a supervisor, a student, a concerned citizen? What would my reader expect from a person in my position?
4. How much background information does this reader need?

If you are writing a movie review for a local newspaper, for instance, you can assume that your readers are movie-goers who want to know whether this movie is worth seeing. Since your readers haven't seen the movie, they will expect you to provide a brief summary of the plot and to comment on the strengths and weaknesses of the story, the acting, and the direction. Because you are writing for non-specialist readers, you would not use specialized technical terms to describe camera angles, lighting, or special effects.

If you are writing an essay on a movie as part of a film course, however, you can make quite different assumptions about your reader. For one thing, because your instructor has already seen the film, you don't need to summarize the plot. Instead, your instructor wants to know your interpretation of the movie. In explaining your interpretation, you will use specialized technical terms, partly to show that you understand their meaning, but primarily because they allow you to be more precise about the film's strengths and weaknesses.

As you can see, the perspective from which you gather, sort, and develop information depends partly on your purpose (to explain, to share personal experience, to persuade), partly on your subject, and partly on the needs of a particular reader. It takes practice to make these adjustments. Here are some exercises to help you get started. You can use these questions as a model for formulating more specific questions about particular readers.

Exercises

Directions: Construct reader profiles for each of the following situations by briefly answering the questions.

Situation 1

Suppose that you are giving an account of your educational background and work experience for a prospective employer. To get a sense of the needs and interests of this reader, ask yourself these questions:

1. Who is my reader?
2. What would a person in this position need and want to know?
3. What skills and abilities would this reader look for in a prospective employee?
4. What aspects of my educational background and work experience should I emphasize?

Situation 2

Suppose that you are living in a community that is two kilometres from a proposed site for a new city dump. As the spokesperson for this community, you have the responsibility of writing to the mayor opposing this proposal. Ask yourself these questions about your reader:

1. What would a mayor be mainly interested in? getting votes? balancing the needs of residents in different areas of the city? costs?
2. What would a mayor expect from the spokesperson for a group opposed to the proposed dump site?
3. How much background information does the mayor need about the concerns of this group?
4. What assumptions can I make about the mayor's position?
5. What kinds of arguments are most likely to appeal to the mayor?

Situation 3

Now suppose that you are the representative from city council appointed by the mayor to convince the residents of this community to accept the proposed dump site. You know they are opposed to it. Ask yourself these questions to get a clearer sense of your audience:

1. What kinds of people live in this neighbourhood? What kinds of work do they do? What is their educational background? What is their income level? Has this community had to cope with other hardships?
2. What does this community expect from the mayor's office?
3. Why would the residents probably not want a dump located near their community?
4. What kinds of arguments would appeal to these residents?

Situation 4

Assume that you are a student in an introductory English literature course. You have been asked to write your first essay assignment. To get a sense of the assumptions you can make about your instructor, ask yourself these questions:

1. What would an instructor look for in the content of an essay about literature?
2. What expectations does this instructor have about essay format?
3. What clues would an essay topic give me about what the instructor expects in this assignment?

2
Paragraph Structure

Sometimes you will write paragraphs that are separate pieces of writing, complete in themselves. However, most often you'll write paragraphs as parts of longer pieces of writing. For instance, a report on absenteeism at your workplace might include several paragraphs, each making a different point about one part of the problem. In this report you could use one paragraph to provide statistical evidence that absenteeism is increasing, another paragraph to discuss reasons for absenteeism, and yet another to recommend solutions to the problem. As you can see, each paragraph focuses on one part of the broad subject and develops that part with specific information.

Organizing and developing paragraphs effectively is an important part of organizing and developing longer pieces of writing such as essays, reports, and letters. The following guidelines will help you to understand the components of a good paragraph.

Topic Sentences

[*Forms of Writing*, Part 2: 4a]

In order to help your reader see the point you are making in a paragraph, you will usually express that point in one sentence called a **topic sentence**. A good topic sentence gives your reader a clear understanding of what the paragraph is about. If the topic sentence begins the paragraph, your reader will even be able to anticipate some of the ideas you will develop in the paragraph.

Because you want the topic sentence to establish the point of the paragraph, statements of fact do not make good topic sentences. An opening topic sentence such as *Many people own pet goldfish* merely states a fact. It doesn't give any indication of what the paragraph will say about owning a goldfish. However, a topic sentence such as *A goldfish makes an ideal household pet* does make a point about the subject. In this case the point is that there are advantages to owning a goldfish. This topic sentence also clearly controls the content of the paragraph; your reader knows that the paragraph will focus only on why a goldfish makes a good pet.

Exercise 1

Put a check mark beside each statement that would make a good topic sentence for a paragraph. Remember that a topic sentence makes a clear point about the subject of the paragraph.

1. If you follow these five steps, you'll be able to change a flat tire with ease.
2. The belief that families have traditionally consisted of a father who acts as sole breadwinner and a mother who stays home to raise the children has little basis in historical fact.
3. I have a friend who lives in Inuvik.
4. Living next door to the Adams family is like living next door to a house of horrors.
5. People are permitted to smoke only in designated areas of the building.
6. In Canada, November 11 is Remembrance Day; in the United States, November 11 is Veterans' Day.
7. Being alone with my thoughts helps me to find solutions to many of my problems.
8. Some people interfere in other people's business.
9. Jumping to conclusions can lead to misunderstanding and hurt feelings.
10. On Christmas Day we had sleet and freezing rain.

Exercise 2

The following statements do not make good topic sentences because they are simply statements of fact. Revise each so that it makes a point about the subject.

1. Many people in Canada watch professional hockey games.
2. The small sailboat overturned during the storm.
3. A pit bull is a breed of dog.
4. The maple leaf flag was declared Canada's official flag on February 15, 1965.
5. The people in the next apartment play their stereo very loudly.

Exercise 3

Below are specific goals for three different paragraphs. Write an effective topic sentence for each paragraph.

1. GOAL   to explain how to eat with chopsticks

   TOPIC SENTENCE _____

2. GOAL   to persuade my readers to use public transportation

   TOPIC SENTENCE _____

3. GOAL   to describe the sense of loss I felt when my best friend moved away

   TOPIC SENTENCE _____

Structuring a Paragraph

[*Forms of Writing,* Part 2: 4b]

The two basic patterns for organizing ideas in a paragraph are **deductive** and **inductive**. In a **deductive paragraph** you write the topic sentence at or very near the beginning and then provide details to expand on your point. In a paragraph about the advantages of owning a pet goldfish, for example, you could begin with the main point that owning a goldfish does not require a major investment of money and time. You would then develop this point by showing how inexpensive and easy it is to care for a goldfish. The paragraph below follows such a deductive pattern. The topic sentence has been underlined.

> <u>For people who do not wish to devote large amounts of money and time to the care and feeding of a pet, a goldfish makes an ideal choice.</u> One advantage of owning a goldfish is that the pet itself costs very little, the least expensive selling for around fifty cents. The price of the bowl will depend on the size and style, but an attractive one can be had for only a few dollars. Additional decorative touches such as sand and small ornaments for the bottom of the bowl require only a minimal further investment. As well, it costs only pennies to fill the bowl each time the water is changed. In addition to being inexpensive, a goldfish is very easy to care for. Feeding, for example, is almost effortless. There's no need to struggle with difficult-to-open, messy cans. It's a simple matter to flip the lid on a container of fish food and shake the food into the bowl once or twice a day. Even better is the fact that a fish never has to be housebroken or taken for walks, never has to be groomed or dewormed, and never has to attend obedience classes. And the little creature makes few demands for affection. In return for an occasional smile and the odd kind word, a goldfish will remain a loyal, steadfast companion.

In an **inductive paragraph**, on the other hand, the supporting details come first. The reader moves through these details to the main point expressed at the end of the paragraph. The inductive paragraph below presents a series of details about the advantages of owning a goldfish before stating the main point in the topic sentence, the underlined final sentence in the paragraph.

Of all pets, with the possible exception of the earthworm, the goldfish is the least expensive to purchase and maintain. The basic model costs around fifty cents; for an additional few dollars the owner can buy a simple goldfish bowl and optional decorative items such as sand and small ornaments for the bottom of the bowl. Keeping the water fresh costs only pennies each time the bowl is filled. Not only is a goldfish inexpensive, but it is also very easy to care for. Feeding, for example, is a simple matter of flipping the lid on a container of fish food once or twice a day and shaking the food into the bowl. Nor does a fish owner ever have to housebreak or walk the pet, groom or deworm it, or take it to obedience classes. Finally, a goldfish makes few emotional demands on its owner. In return for an occasional smile and the odd kind word, a goldfish will remain a loyal and steadfast companion. <u>For people unwilling to spend a great deal of money and time on a pet, a goldfish is the ideal choice.</u>

Exercise 1

Label each of the following paragraphs *D* for deductive organization or *I* for inductive organization. Underline the topic sentence in each.

1. As the Bible says, "To everything there is a season, and a time to every purpose under heaven." More specifically, there's a time to say what is on your mind and a time to let the moment pass. When a friend's new perm makes her look like a poodle with its paw in a light socket, bear in mind that an honest expression of your opinion will do nothing for your friend's self-esteem or for the friendship. If you can't say something nice, say something vague, like "I've never seen your hair look so full and bouncy." Let her interpret the comment as she will. And if you're ever in the awkward position of having to choke down a host's highly unpalatable meal, refrain from analyzing the reasons that the meat is so tough and the vegetables so soggy. Your critique will not be viewed as an expression of friendly concern about cooking techniques. Instead, talk about your host's elegant table or his exquisite taste in dinner rolls and wine. He'll appreciate your discretion. Just remember—he had to eat the meal, too.

2. Have you ever been enraged at a brother or sister who took something of yours without asking? Have you ever hurled insults at a sibling

whom at that moment you regarded as the stupidest person on earth? Have you ever fought vehemently in defence of that same sibling when he or she was insulted or hurt by someone else? The fact that you fight with brothers and sisters does not necessarily mean that you do not care for them.

3. Some parents always pick up after their children; always drive them to school, to music lessons, to the playground; always step in to settle arguments with young friends. Some parents make all the important decisions for their kids—how they'll spend their spare time, what school courses they'll take, what careers they'll follow. The problem with this approach is that children who are not taught to assume responsibility for themselves and for their decisions will have difficulty acting responsibly when they grow up. Parents who exert too much control over a child's life will hinder the child's growth to maturity.

4. I hereby plead guilty to the charge of not always putting my time to productive use; in fact, I admit that I actually enjoy wasting time. I know when the windows need washing, but I can't resist the call of the hammock on a sunny afternoon. I can see the snow on the sidewalk, but I can easily ignore the shovel in favour of a few rousing games of solitaire. Certainly I recognize the need for keeping up in my courses, but I suffer withdrawal symptoms without my fix of television "soap" for an hour every day. I am shameless. I feel no guilt as I squander the precious gift of time in pleasing but trivial pursuits.

Exercise 2

Using the following kinds of movie-goers as a basis, write a deductively organized paragraph on the way people behave at the movies. You can expand on the information by adding more details. Then rewrite the paragraph so that the organization is inductive. In both paragraphs you will need an effective topic sentence.

- people who arrive late at the movie theatre and step on toes as they make their way to a centre seat
- people who fidget and kick the seat in front of them
- people who chomp loudly on candy and popcorn and slurp noisily on drinks
- people who talk throughout the movie

Keeping Your Focus Clear

As you know, the topic sentence controls the content of a paragraph. In a clearly focused paragraph all the information relates to the point about the subject expressed in the topic sentence. If you introduce unrelated information, the paragraph will lack focus and your reader will have difficulty following your train of thought. In the deductive paragraph below, notice that several sentences do not develop the point about advertising appeals made in the topic sentence.

Advertising companies use a number of appeals to entice us into buying their clients' products. Radio advertising is a particularly effective and inexpensive way of reaching a large audience. In commercials for such appliances as microwave ovens and electric dishwashers, for instance, advertisers appeal to our desire for convenience, specifically the convenience of getting chores done with a minimum investment of time and effort. The prices of microwave ovens have dropped significantly in the past few years. Advertisers also appeal to our desire for comfort, as is evident in ads for products ranging from running shoes to carpets to recliner rockers. However, perhaps the most pervasive appeal is that made to our desire for social acceptance. In some people, the need to belong is much stronger than in others. We'll be part of the "in" crowd, the ads imply, if we drink the right cola or beer. Fortunately, there are television commercials warning people against drinking and driving. We'll look younger if we use the right skin care products, thinner if we follow the right diet plan, and sexier if we brush with the right toothpaste. As the ads tell us relentlessly, the more we conform to the advertisers' conception of beauty, the more desirable others will find us.

Read through the paragraph again and cross out the sentences that put the paragraph "off track." The revised paragraph reads as follows:

Advertising companies use a number of appeals to entice us into buying their clients' products. In commercials for such appliances as microwave ovens and electric dishwashers, for instance, advertisers appeal to our desire for convenience, specifically the convenience of getting chores done with a minimum investment of time and effort. Advertisers also appeal to our desire for comfort, as is evident in ads for products ranging from running shoes to carpets to recliner rockers. However, perhaps the most pervasive appeal is that made to our desire for social acceptance. We'll be part of the "in" crowd, the ads imply, if we drink the right cola or beer. We'll look younger if we use the right skin care products, thinner if we follow the right diet plan, and sexier if we brush with the right toothpaste. As the ads tell us relentlessly, the more we conform to the advertisers' conception of beauty, the more desirable others will find us.

In the following deductively organized narrative, the details stay in focus until near the end. Mark where the shift in focus occurs.

Getting ready to give my first public speech was the most nerve-wracking experience of my life. I had been asked by a group of local business managers to discuss the work of the environmental action committee to which I belong. I worked frantically, writing and revising the speech countless times, shaping the ideas into what I hoped was an intelligent, informative, and interesting presentation. As I prepared, I was plagued by self-doubt and fear. What if I did so poorly that I embarrassed myself and my organization? As the day for the speech drew closer, my nervousness increased. I existed in a fog, oblivious to all around me. I couldn't eat. I couldn't sleep. At times I even had trouble breathing. When the day itself arrived, the fear escalated to panic. I was in such a lather that I had to shower twice and change my shirt three times. Then I was driving to the auditorium; I was entering the building; I was approaching the podium, my notes clutched in my sweaty palm, my throat constricting in terror. However, I need not have worried. After a few nervous moments, a wonderful calm came over me, and I delivered the speech flawlessly. The business managers were so pleased with my presentation that I've been asked to speak to them again.

According to the topic sentence, the point of the paragraph is that the writer lived in a state of fear as he prepared for his first public speaking engagement. All the details support this point until the writer gets to the sentence, "However, I need not have worried." The rest of the paragraph focuses not on the writer's fear but on his success. This new material should be covered in a separate paragraph. In your own paragraphs, be sure to keep all the supporting details in line with the topic sentence.

Developing Your Ideas Fully

[Forms of Writing, Part 2: 5-6]

In any paragraph you should provide enough interesting, concrete, vivid detail to give your reader a solid understanding of the point you are making about your subject. Remember that your reader did not go through the thinking process involved in writing the paper and therefore will not have all the ideas you sifted through in producing the final draft. If you do not get the supporting details down on paper, you cannot expect your reader to fill in the blanks. Remember also that repeating an idea several times in different words is not an effective way of developing a paragraph, as you can see in the following example.

16

A well-balanced diet will include a variety of nutritious foods. When planning meals, be sure to select items from different food groups. Without such variety, you will not get all the nutrients that should be part of a balanced diet.

Every sentence in the paragraph makes the same point: that a balanced diet is based on eating a variety of foods. The paragraph below develops the idea more fully by giving specific examples of the foods that should be part of a balanced diet.

A well-balanced diet will include a variety of nutritious foods from each of the four food groups outlined in Canada's Food Guide. The Guide recommends at least three servings a day from the fruits and vegetables group. Choices include oranges, apples, tomatoes, broccoli, carrots, potatoes, and spinach. The Guide also recommends three to five daily servings of breads and cereals, such as whole grain bread, ready-to-eat cereal, oatmeal, rice, and pasta. Adults need about 500 millilitres (2 cups) a day of milk and milk products such as cheese and yogurt. Finally, adults should also have two daily servings of meat, fish, poultry, or alternatives such as lentils and beans. These recommended foods provide the vitamins, minerals, and other nutrients necessary for good health.

In *Forms of Writing*, you will find guidelines for writing a number of different kinds of paragraphs. Use these guidelines to help you develop your ideas fully.

Making Your Writing Flow

In addition to being clearly focused and adequately developed, a good paragraph creates a sense of continuity. One sentence leads smoothly into the next, and the connections between ideas are clear. Without this continuity, the paragraph can seem choppy and disjointed, as is the case in the following example.

[Forms of Writing, Revising 1]

Urban myths are fascinating examples of modern folklore. Often these stories are anecdotes about a frightening or shocking incident. The teller firmly believes the story to be true. Before beginning, the teller will make a statement. She will say that the incident really did happen to someone she knows or knows of. This statement makes the story even more shocking. For example, a young woman is driving home alone on a dark country road. She sees a man waving frantically at the side of the road. He is signalling her to stop. She stops but remains in the car. The man approaches. The young woman cautiously lowers the window an inch or two. In the rear view mirror she sees another man. He is swinging a huge chain at her back window. She immediately puts the car into gear and peels away. She arrives home, and still shaking, she gets out of the car to inspect the damage. To her horror she sees a piece of chain. It is wrapped around the back bumper. Caught in one link of the chain is a man's finger.

This paragraph provides enough detail, and all of the details are relevant. However, the ideas don't flow together smoothly, largely because there are too many simple sentences and not enough transitional words and phrases to guide the reader. The revised version below is much smoother and easier to follow.

Urban myths are fascinating examples of modern folklore. Often these stories are anecdotes about frightening or shocking incidents that the teller firmly believes to be true. Indeed, before beginning, the teller will preface the story with a statement that the incident really did happen to someone he or she knows or knows of. It is this affirmation of the tale's truth that makes it even more shocking. In one such story, for example, a young woman is said to be driving home alone on a dark country road when she is signalled to stop by a man waving frantically at the side of the road. She does stop but remains in the car. As the man approaches, the young woman cautiously lowers the window an inch or two. Suddenly, in the rear view mirror she sees another man swinging a huge chain at her back window. She immediately puts the car into gear and peels away. When she arrives home, still shaking, she gets out of the car to inspect the damage. To her horror she sees a piece of chain wrapped around the back bumper. Caught in one link of the chain is a man's finger.

Through subordination and transitional expressions you can help your reader see how the ideas in a paragraph are connected. You will find a more complete discussion of these techniques in *Forms of Writing*, Revising 1: Making Your Writing Flow. Here are just a few of the transitional words and phrases that can give your writing a sense of continuity.

SPATIAL RELATIONSHIPS	up, down; at the front, at the back; beside, on top of, in the middle, underneath; nearby, farther away; inside, outside.
TIME RELATIONSHIPS	at first, afterwards, in the meantime, while, when, finally; at the start of, at the end of; last month, next week, this year.
ADDITION	and; in addition, moreover.
CAUSE/EFFECT	therefore, consequently, as a result; so, because.
CONTRAST	but, yet; however, on the other hand.

Exercise

In each group of sentences below, the sentences are connected, but the ideas do not flow together smoothly. Add transitional words or phrases or use subordination to make the relationships between ideas clear.

1. We lost most of the apple blossoms to a late spring snowstorm. We can expect a small apple harvest.

   _____

2. Mr. Woo waited for Stephen in the boardroom. Stephen was trapped between floors in a stalled elevator.

   _____

3. The lead is played by an actress of considerable skill and sensitivity. Her talents cannot bring this one-dimensional character to life.

   _____

4. The lumber was left uncovered in the rain. It warped badly. Very few pieces are usable.

   _____

5. Vivian looked across the lawn. She was startled to see Marvin standing beside the gazebo, his face white, his fists clenched. There was a crumpled piece of paper. Arnold, who had apparently acted as messenger, stood there. Marvin raised his fist—to signal despair or to strike Arnold?

   _____

   _____

6. Marika tried to start the car. She discovered that the battery was dead. She got out of the car. She dropped her briefcase. The latch immediately sprang open. The contents spilled into a large mud puddle. Marika remained calm.

   _____

   _____

7. Ramon smothered the pizza dough in tomato sauce. He heaped on slices of pepperoni and back bacon, shrimps, green peppers, black olives, and red onion. He piled shredded mozzarella over all. He put the monstrous concoction into the waiting oven.

   _____

   _____

8. Luis heard his name announced over the car radio. He sped up slightly and began searching for a pay phone. If he could call the station within ten minutes, he would win an all-expenses paid trip to Vancouver. He approached the stop sign. He slowed down. Without coming to a complete stop, he proceeded across the intersection. A police siren started up behind him.

_____

_____

9. A grease fire started in the frying pan. It flared up. It ignited the curtains hanging near the stove. It spread to the dish towel lying on the counter.

_____

_____

10. A painting or a sculpture is a tangible, enduring record of the artist's creative power. Movies are enduring records of artistic expression. Each time the movie is run, the performances come to life exactly as they were created at the moment of filming. A live performance of dance, music, or theatre is ephemeral. Those few hours of creative expression end with the final curtain, never to be recreated in precisely the same way.

_____

_____

3
Practice in Writing Paragraphs

Writing Situation 1: Writing a Paragraph to Explain: Process Analysis

[*Forms of Writing*, Part 2: 5e]

In this expository paragraph assignment, your goal is to explain how to carry out a particular procedure. Imagine that you have been asked to write this paragraph for a guest column in a weekly community newspaper. Choose one of the following topics:

1. how to have a miserable time at a party
2. how to ask someone for a date
3. how to roller-skate for the first time
4. how to spend a lazy Sunday afternoon
5. a topic of your choice

Preparing

1. After choosing your topic, write your specific goal by completing the sentence *My goal in this piece is to explain how to* _____.
2. Make a list of the steps involved in completing the process. Read over the list, adding new steps if necessary. Number the steps in order from first to last.

Drafting

1. Write a topic sentence that makes a point about the procedure, such as the fact that your readers will find it useful.

2. Write out all the steps in the procedure in complete sentences, in chronological order, using proper paragraph format. Since you are explaining the procedure directly to your readers, you should address them with the pronouns *you* and *your*. You may also use command sentences such as this one describing a step in topic 3: *Before going to the roller-skating rink, be sure that your life and health insurance policies are up-to-date.*

Revising

1. As you read over the draft, ask yourself these questions:
    a) Does my topic sentence make a point about the procedure?
    b) Are the steps arranged in a logical order?
    c) Have I provided enough detail to make the procedure clear?
    d) Are the connections between the steps clear? Have I used transitions such as *first, next, after, when, finally* to make the paragraph flow?
2. Rewrite your expository paragraph, making any necessary changes.
3. Proofread your work carefully. If you need help with grammar and sentence structure, see the relevant sections in the workbook and the text.

[*Forms of Writing*, Part 2: 6c]

Writing Situation 2: Writing a Paragraph to Share Personal Experience: The Analogy

An **analogy** is an extended comparison between two apparently quite dissimilar things—marriage and a card game, love and a freeway, the city and the jungle. An analogy can be a useful way of explaining something because it is often easier for a reader to understand one thing when you compare it to another. For this reason, analogies work best when you can explain something unfamiliar by comparing it with something more familiar.

To give yourself practice writing analogies, imagine that you are trying to explain an experience with which your reader is unfamiliar. Explain this experience in a paragraph of about 300 words by comparing your experience with one your reader is likely to understand. Introduce your analogy with a simile (a comparison using *like* or *as*).

Examples
Coping with a serious illness is like moonlighting with a second job.
My first Christmas with my in-laws was like a visit to a foreign country.

Preparing

1. Write 3-5 similes. Be sure the things you are comparing are different enough to be developed as an analogy. *Having a new baby is like having twice as much to do,* for instance, will not work as the opening simile for an analogy.
2. Choose the most promising simile and freewrite for five minutes.
3. If your comparison falls apart as you try to extend it, choose another simile and start again.

Drafting

Write a paragraph developing the comparison set out in your best simile. Use your simile as your topic sentence.

Revising

1. As you read over your draft, ask yourself these questions:
    a) Is the analogy appropriate?
    b) Is the paragraph clearly focused? Does all of the material used to develop the analogy fit with the initial simile? Does any of it seem out of place?
    c) Does the paragraph have a sense of continuity? Does it include transitions that move the reader smoothly from point to point? Are the connections between my ideas clear?
2. Revise your analogy, making any necessary changes .
3. Proofread your work carefully. If you need help with specific points of grammar and sentence structure, check the relevant sections of the workbook and the text.

Writing Situation 3: Writing a Paragraph to Share Personal Experience: Personal Definition

[*Forms of Writing,* Part 2: 6a]

When you write a **personal definition**, your purpose is to explain what an abstract concept, such as *home, marriage,* or *travel,* means to you. To develop your personal definition, you would share experiences associated with *home* or *marriage* or *travel* with your readers.

Most of us, for example, have had the unpleasant experience of being an outsider, so we feel that we understand what the term *outsider* means. What would you say, however, if you were asked to define what this word means to you?

For this assignment, write a paragraph defining what the word *outsider* means to you. If defining *outsider* doesn't appeal to you, consult with your instructor and choose another word.

Preparing

Put the word *outsider* in the middle of the page. Around it, put the thoughts and feelings that this word evokes for you.

Drafting

1. Begin with a sentence defining *outsider*.

   To me, being an outsider means _____.

2. Fill out some of these thoughts and feelings with specific examples to make them clearer and more vivid for your reader. You may want to include negative examples (what being an outsider does *not* mean).

3. Sometimes an analogy can be an effective method for developing a personal definition. An analogy is an extended comparison in which you explain something unfamiliar by comparing it with something familiar. If you want to develop your personal definition as an analogy, you will need to begin your paragraph with a simile (a comparison using *like* or *as*: *Being an outsider is like...*).

[*Forms of Writing,* Part 2: 6c]

Revising

1. As you read over your draft, ask yourself these questions:
   a) Does my paragraph begin with a topic sentence defining *outsider*?
   b) Are my examples clear and relevant? If the definition is developed as an analogy, does everything in the paragraph fit with the opening simile?
   c) Is the definition complete?
2. Rewrite your personal definition essay, making any necessary changes.
3. Proofread your work carefully. Pay particular attention to errors identified in other pieces of writing. If you need help, consult the relevant sections of the workbook and the text.

Writing Situation 4: Writing a Paragraph to Persuade: Evaluation

[*Forms of Writing*, Part 2: 6d; Revising 8]

Your goal in this paragraph is to persuade your readers to change their behaviour by agreeing to do what you ask of them in the paragraph. Choose one of the following topics.

1. You are the campaign manager for a friend who is running for president of the students' association. Write a paragraph for a campaign flyer urging fellow students to vote for your candidate.
2. A relative who has just opened a new restaurant has asked you to write a short advertising feature for a local newspaper. Your relative wants you to praise the food and the service.
3. A colleague at work has applied for a position with another company and has asked you to write a brief letter of recommendation. Write a paragraph convincing the personnel manager of the other company that your colleague is an excellent candidate for the position.
4. An obnoxious out-of-town relative plans to spend a month at your place in the summer. Without putting too great a strain on family harmony, write a short letter convincing your relative that his or her plans will have to be changed.
5. A topic of your choice [Describe the situation that prompts you to write the paragraph.]

Preparing

1. Write your specific goal by completing the sentence *My goal in this piece is to convince my reader(s) to _____*.
2. Make a list of reasons, examples, or other information that can answer your audience's question, *Why should I do what you want?* (*Why should I vote for your candidate? Why should I eat at that restaurant? Why should I consider this applicant for the job? Why should I change my vacation plans?*)
3. Read over your list and choose the strongest three or four ideas. Arrange them in order from least important to most important.

Drafting

1. Write a topic sentence that expresses an opinion about your subject, such as *I recommend Sharon Cohen as an excellent candidate for the position of sales agent with your company.*
2. Write out your three or four strongest reasons, beginning with the least

important. Provide enough detail to make your reasons clear to your reader.
3. If you find that the paragraph ends too abruptly after your last reason, write a concluding sentence that sums up your main point.

Revising

1. As you read over your work, ask yourself these questions:
   a) Have I stated an opinion in my topic sentence?
   b) Have I arranged my ideas from least to most important? Have I used sufficient detail to convince my readers to do what I want them to do?
   c) Have I used transitional words and expressions, or other devices, to make the connections between sentences clear?
2. Rewrite your persuasive paragraph, making any necessary changes.
3. Proofread your work carefully. Check the relevant sections of the workbook and the text for help with grammar and sentence structure.

4
Essays and
Related Forms

Discovering a Thesis

An **essay** is a short piece of non-fiction writing that makes a point about its subject. Newspaper columns, magazine articles, and research papers are all examples of essays. More material can be covered in an essay than in a paragraph. A paragraph on the subject of travel, for instance, might explain how to book a vacation trip through a travel agent. In an essay on travel, you could explore the subject in much more depth. For instance, you might explain how to travel in Europe on a shoe-string budget. A paragraph on making plans through a travel agent would be only one part of your essay.

[*Forms of Writing*, Part 3: 7]

The point that you make about your subject in an essay is called the **thesis**. When you know a great deal about your subject, you may already have a point or thesis before you begin to write. For example, if you have experience working with mentally handicapped people and believe very strongly that they should not be segregated in institutions, you could begin an essay with that point in mind. You would express your thesis in a sentence such as *Integrating developmentally delayed people into the larger community by placing them in group homes will benefit both those individuals and society as a whole.* In the rest of the essay, you would develop paragraphs through reasons, descriptions, examples, or other details to show what these advantages are.

In other writing situations, however, you may not know exactly what you want to say about your subject. The writing process will be a way for you to learn more about your subject and to clarify your thinking. In this case, how do you finally decide on a focus?

Suppose that you have been asked to write an essay on day care. Before you begin, you need to gather material on the subject. You will already have some ideas that you can explore through brainstorming or freewriting. Some of this knowledge may be based on what you have already read on the subject or on experiences you may have had with putting your own children into a day care centre. You can acquire more information through research—by reading books and articles and by interviewing day care workers and parents. When you have sufficient material, you need to determine how to arrange the ideas into manageable units. Let's say you have come up with the following list of ideas about day care centres. Can you take related ideas and group them into broader categories? Go through this list and sort out the ideas into categories. As a start, use *cost* as one category.

1. academic qualifications of staff (current first aid certificate, post-secondary courses or diploma in early childhood development)
2. layout of facilities (playing, sleeping, cooking, eating areas; washrooms; nursery area for infants)
3. personal qualities of staff (empathic, supportive)
4. cleanliness, safety
5. monthly rates per child
6. games, toys, books
7. cost of additional equipment, materials, clothing (e.g., sleeping mat, paint smock)
8. proximity of centre to parents' home or place of employment
9. field trips and outings for children
10. additional expenses for outings
11. arts and crafts

Here is one suggestion for arranging the material:

a) cost (5, 7, 10)
b) facilities (2, 4, 8)
c) staff (1, 3)
d) activities for children (6, 9, 11)

Grouping your ideas into categories this way is an important step in determining your thesis. However, it is not the only step; you also have to decide on your purpose and audience and on the method of development. How you express your thesis and what ideas you include in the essay will depend on all these factors. Notice the differences in a thesis for an expository, a personal, and a persuasive essay on day care in the following examples.

TYPE OF ESSAY	THESIS
Expository (Analysis) Goal: to explain to parents how to choose a good day care centre	If you are a working parent, you know the importance of good day care. In choosing the best day care centre for your child, consider the cost, the quality of the facilities, the professional and personal qualifications of the staff, and the activities provided for the children.
Personal Goal: to tell what happened when I went in search of the perfect day care centre	When I decided to go back to school full-time, I had to put my toddler into day care. Finding an affordable day care centre that met my criteria of excellent facilities, a supportive staff, and stimulating activities for the children proved to be a very difficult challenge.
Persuasive Goal: to convince parents that day care centres can provide a stimulating environment for their children	A high-quality day care centre staffed by supportive care givers will provide a stimulating environment that meets the cognitive, emotional, and social needs of your child.

Discovering a Thesis for a Comparison Essay

A thesis statement like *These two things have a lot in common* or *There are many differences between these two things* does not get an essay developed through comparison off to a good start. To formulate a good thesis for a comparison essay, you need to decide what point you want to make about your subjects. If you were comparing dogs and cats as house pets, for example, you might want to focus on the amount of care they need or on the amount of affection they give an owner. By making a point about either care or affection, you can establish a basis of comparison that enables you to see what belongs in your essay and what you can leave out.

[*Forms of Writing*, Part 3: 7a-b]

Exercise 1

A good thesis statement makes a point about the subject and provides control over the rest of the essay. Put a check mark beside each statement that could serve as an effective thesis for an essay. Be prepared to explain the weakness of each statement you did not check.

1. Tracing your genealogy requires persistence and hard work, but the rewards of understanding your family and yourself through understanding the past are well worth the effort.
2. The Gregorian calendar, a correction of the Julian calendar, was introduced by Pope Gregory XIII in 1582.
3. That day I learned my most valuable swimming lesson: never to turn my back on the ocean.
4. Seeing the movie and reading the book are two quite different experiences.
5. We may pay lip service to such adages as "Never judge a book by its cover" and "The clothes don't make the man," but the reality of corporate life is that we will be judged by the way we dress.
6. Many people enjoy periods of solitude.
7. The stresses of living in a small town are quite different from the stresses of living in a large city.
8. Being a truly dedicated couch potato is not easy, but if you're ready to face the hardships and the sacrifice, the following guidelines will help you to achieve your goal.
9. The *Titanic* struck an iceberg on April 14, 1912, and sank in less than three hours. The wreck was discovered off the coast of Newfoundland in 1985.
10. Collecting baseball cards and comic books isn't a kids' game anymore. Today's collector is often more interested in future profits than in fun.

Exercise 2

Write a specific goal and formulate a thesis for a personal essay based on the following scenario.

My boss asked me to work one Saturday in February. Because I had been planning for some time to go skiing with friends that weekend, I asked for the time off, but my boss said she couldn't spare me. On the Saturday morning I phoned in sick and went skiing anyway. Whom should I happen to see skiing at the same resort but my boss! As she skied past me on the intermediate slope, she called out, "Be there bright and early Monday morning to clean out your desk. You're fired."

Making an Outline

In deciding how to plan the first draft of an essay, you must choose the technique that works best for you. Some writers do not have a clear thesis or definite plan in mind before they begin a paper. Instead, they use the writing process itself as a means of discovering what they want to say about the subject. They write a draft to allow their thoughts to emerge. Then they formulate their thesis and write further drafts, reworking and reorganizing their material until the essay most effectively expresses their ideas.

Other writers may use the technique described in the preceding section, "Discovering a Thesis." After generating ideas, grouping the ideas into broad categories, and writing their thesis, they can establish a guideline for organization by writing topic sentences for middle paragraphs. In this way they can keep the focus of the entire paper and of each section clearly in mind. For more information on relating topic sentences to a thesis, see the following section, "Deductive Pattern: Thesis and Topic Sentences."

Still other writers prefer to devise a **formal outline** to help them organize the supporting details before they begin the first draft. If you want to work out the structure of your essay in this way, you can make a formal outline by labelling major points with Roman numerals (I, II, III), subpoints with capital letters (A, B, C), and specific examples with Arabic numerals (1, 2, 3). Express items within each section in parallel grammatical form. Here is how you would make a formal outline for an essay on fitness.

THESIS: A good fitness program includes regular exercise, a balanced diet, and techniques for coping with stress.

I. Exercise
  A. Stretching exercises
    1. arms
    2. legs
    3. waist
  B. Aerobic exercises
    1. rowing
    2. brisk walking or jogging
    3. bicycling
    4. aerobics classes
  C. Strengthening and toning exercises
    1. arms
    2. legs
    3. abdominals

II. Diet
  A. Foods to avoid
    1. fat
    2. cholesterol
    3. sugar
    4. salt
  B. Foods to eat
    1. fruits and vegetables
    2. meats and alternatives
    3. breads and cereals
    4. milk and milk products
III. Stress-reduction techniques
  A. Breathing exercises
  B. Physical relaxation exercises
  C. Mental relaxation exercises

Note that in a formal outline, when you have a subsection A, you must also have a subsection B. When you have an example 1, you must also have an example 2. The reason is that an outline is a type of classification system. It is a way of classifying points. If you want to divide a major point such as *exercise* into more specific types of exercises, you need to create two or more subcategories, i.e., to describe two or more types of exercises. It's not possible to divide *exercise* into only one subsection on, say, stretching exercises. If you can create only one subcategory, there is no point in making the division in the first place. In fact, if you want to give examples only of stretching exercises, *stretching exercises* should be the broad category.

Exercise

Using the material on day care centres (pp. 28-29) make a formal outline for an expository or persuasive essay on the subject. If you wish, you may generate more ideas before you begin. Write your thesis (either one of the examples given or your own version) at the top of the page. Then label major points with Roman numerals, subpoints with capitals, and any examples with Arabic numerals.

Essay Structure

The two basic patterns for organizing an essay are **deductive** and **inductive**. Because most essays you write in college and university courses will follow a deductive pattern of organization, we will concentrate on this method of development.

Deductive Pattern: Thesis and Topic Sentences

[*Forms of Writing*, Part 3: 8a]

As you are gathering material for your essay and deciding on the major categories for organizing the information, you can work out a tentative thesis that will tell your readers what categories you will develop and the order in which you will discuss them. Suppose, for instance, that you are writing an essay on fitness according to the outline given. Your major categories would be exercise, diet, and stress-reduction techniques. Your thesis would mention these categories in the order in which you plan to discuss them:

A good fitness program includes regular exercise, a balanced diet, and techniques for coping with stress.

Because you have chosen a deductive method of development, this thesis will appear in the introduction to the essay. A major advantage of placing your thesis at the beginning is that your readers will know the main point of the essay at the outset and can more easily follow your discussion as you develop this main point through examples, reasons, and other details.

As a further guide to your readers, each middle paragraph in a deductive essay should contain a topic sentence that clearly connects the paragraph to your thesis. You can make the connection by having the topic sentence of a paragraph repeat a key word or idea from the thesis. You can see this pattern at work in the following example.

THESIS: A good fitness program includes regular exercise, a balanced diet, and techniques for coping with stress.

TOPIC SENTENCES:

MIDDLE PARAGRAPH #1	Proper exercise is a major component of a good fitness program.
MIDDLE PARAGRAPH #2	In addition to exercising regularly, eating a balanced diet will help you to stay in shape.
MIDDLE PARAGRAPH #3	Finally, keeping fit involves maintaining not only your physical health but also your mental health through dealing effectively with stress in your life.

Working out a precise thesis and such clearly connected topic sentences isn't easy on the first try, but your ideas will come more clearly into focus as you work on the draft of the paper. If you find as you are writing your draft that reorganizing the material will result in a more interesting and effective paper, remember that the original thesis isn't written in stone. If you rearrange the material, revise your thesis and topic sentences to reflect your new organization.

Exercise 1

Each of the following items contains a thesis and three possible topic sentences for middle paragraphs. Two of the topic sentences are clearly connected to the thesis. One topic sentence bears some relationship to the subject, but it is not clearly connected to the thesis. Put an X beside the ineffective topic sentence; then write a good topic sentence to replace it.

1. THESIS: Television is an easily accessible source of entertainment, information, and culture.

TOPIC SENTENCES:

MIDDLE PARAGRAPH #1   One advantage of owning a VCR is that viewers can tape their favourite programs and then zip through the commercials when they play the tape.

MIDDLE PARAGRAPH #2   Television cannot replace books and newspapers, of course, but it can supplement and broaden a viewer's knowledge through news reports, public affairs programs, and documentaries.

MIDDLE PARAGRAPH #3   Viewers are given the opportunity to see televised productions of great theatre, great dance, and great music—cultural experiences they may not otherwise be able to afford.

2. THESIS: When pet owners bring a new puppy home, they take on the responsibilities of feeding and training the animal and of attending to its medical needs.

TOPIC SENTENCES:

MIDDLE PARAGRAPH #1   Responsible dog owners know that their pets cannot thrive on a diet of table scraps; dogs require a nutritious, balanced diet based primarily on commercial pet food.

MIDDLE PARAGRAPH #2   Training a dog to behave acceptably both inside and outside the home requires hard work and discipline on the part of both the owner and the animal.

MIDDLE PARAGRAPH #3   Some dogs have amazing recuperative powers and can recover speedily from illness or injury.

3. THESIS: Good house guests are congenial and considerate, never interfere in the host's affairs, and never overstay their welcome.

TOPIC SENTENCES:

MIDDLE PARAGRAPH #1   Hosts are rightfully upset when a guest takes over the bathroom as his or her personal domain.

MIDDLE PARAGRAPH #2   In addition to being thoughtful, good guests always mind their own business, no matter how tempting it may be to set the host straight on matters of the mind, the heart, or the pocket book.

MIDDLE PARAGRAPH #3   Even the nicest, most unobtrusive guest disrupts a host's routine, so wise visitors keep their stay short and sweet.

Exercise 2

Write three topic sentences for middle paragraphs in an essay based on the following thesis.

> THESIS: Getting a job often depends on how well the interview goes. How well the interview goes may depend on how well you conduct yourself—on how you dress, how you behave, and how you handle the interviewer's questions.

FIRST TOPIC SENTENCE: _____

_____

SECOND TOPIC SENTENCE: _____

_____

THIRD TOPIC SENTENCE: _____

_____

Introduction, Middle Paragraphs, and Conclusion

[*Forms of Writing,* Part 3: 8a]

The Introduction

In a deductively organized essay, the thesis appears at the end of the introduction. The other sentences in the introduction provide a context for the thesis and lead naturally into it. You can establish this context in a variety of ways, among them the following:

1. Make a general statement about the importance of your subject.
2. Provide some historical background for the thesis.
3. Briefly describe an incident or personal experience related to the thesis.
4. Define an important concept on which your thesis is based.
5. Briefly explain an opposing view on your subject that you will refute in the thesis.

The following introduction contains a definition of the word *etiquette* and describes a negative image that the word evokes for many people. The writer then counters with a more positive view of her subject and asserts the importance of good manners—the main point of the essay—in the final sentence.

> For many of us the word *etiquette* conjures up images of stiff, stuffily formal social snobs looking down their noses with disdain at anyone foolish enough to eat salad with the fish fork. Certainly there are those whose good manners are worn merely as a badge of perceived social

superiority. Still, we must not be too ready to dismiss the conventions of polite behaviour as mere symbols of social elitism. Indeed, good manners are ideally a mark of kindness and genuine regard for the feelings of others. The greater the stress in daily life, the greater the need for such manifestations of kindness. Knowing the proper way to behave in given situations makes social interaction smoother and easier for all of us.

The sample introduction below begins by conceding that certain products are very effective in keeping our homes clean. However, the writer then points out the dangers of these products and offers an opposing view, which stresses the need to replace them with safer alternatives.

In our quest for brighter clothes, squeaky clean dishes, and sparkling floors and windows, we have a large array of cleaning agents—bleaches, detergents, industrial-strength cleaners—to aid our cause. However, there is a larger cause to which we must address ourselves. While such products do a superior job of keeping our homes cleaner than clean, they are dangerous pollutants that poison our lakes and rivers. We must take immediate steps to reduce this contamination. Fortunately, with a small investment of time and effort, we can create safer cleaning agents from such readily available products as pure soap, ammonia, washing soda, and vinegar. Using these environmentally friendly cleaners is an important step in helping to reduce the threat that chemical pollution poses to our planet's future.

However you lead into your thesis, make the opening sentences interesting. Avoid mechanical introductions such as *In this essay I will discuss the importance of good manners*. As well, be confident. Don't undermine the strength of your ideas with expressions such as *This paper is an attempt to...* or *It is only my opinion, but I believe that....* In addition, don't make the introduction too long by including detailed information that belongs in the body of the essay. Finally, be sure that all ideas in the introduction are relevant to the thesis. Including unrelated information can mislead your readers about the focus of the essay.

Exercise

Assume that you are writing an essay on one of the theses below. Write an introduction that incorporates the thesis effectively. Remember that the thesis will appear at the end of the introduction and that the other sentences will lead naturally into it.

1. People who love to scare themselves half to death in the comfort of their own homes can rent some truly terrifying videos about ghosts, alien monsters, and deranged killers with a penchant for sharp objects.
2. Both nature and nurture help to shape a person's intellect and personality.
3. Some exercises—in particular sit-ups, knee bends, and leg lifts—are ineffective and even harmful if not done properly.
4. Marriages arranged for young people by their parents, sometimes with the help of a marriage broker, are common in India, Pakistan, and Japan.
5. Scientists continue their efforts to determine whether true communication is possible between humans and such animals as whales, dolphins, and chimpanzees.

Middle Paragraphs

In some essays the material itself determines how you will organize the information in the middle paragraphs. In particular, essays explaining the history of something lend themselves to a chronological arrangement of ideas. A paper on the history of rock music would move from the beginnings of rock to the present. More often, however, there will be several possible ways of arranging your material, and you will have to choose the most effective one. Your aim is to make your discussion clear and interesting to your readers.

The following suggestions will help you achieve that aim.

1. **Move from the easiest to the most difficult concepts:**
In analyzing a past government's policies, you could first discuss social programs, move on to defence policies, and end with economic reforms.

2. **Move from the least significant benefit to the most significant benefit:**
In an essay showing the advantages of using a computer or word processor to write papers, you could begin with the least important benefit by pointing out that the machine will produce a neatly typed final draft. More important, as you would show by discussing this point last, using a computer greatly simplifies the revision process, thereby giving the writer more time and opportunity to improve the quality of thought, the organization, and the writing style in the paper.

3. **Move from the least harmful effect to the most harmful effect:**
A discussion of the problems associated with listening to loud music could begin with the point that a blaring radio or stereo is a major irritant to parents. The most serious problem, which you would leave to the last, is that extended exposure to loud music can lead to hearing loss.

4. Move from the individual person to the larger society:

One way to examine the effects of increased taxation is to move from a discussion of the effects on individual consumers to a discussion of the effects on the national economy.

5. Move from the most practical to the most theoretical or abstract:

A persuasive essay on the benefits of higher education could start with the practical advantage of providing training for better jobs and end with the more abstract advantage of providing a means to greater self-fulfillment.

You'll frequently find that you can't cover a section of material in a single paragraph. If you have too much information for one paragraph, divide it into smaller paragraphs. Make the division where it seems most natural, such as when you move on to another aspect of the category under discussion. You can see this process at work in the following model.

SUBJECT	fitness
FIRST CATEGORY	exercise
SUBSECTIONS	stretching exercises, aerobic exercises, strengthening and toning exercises
FIRST PARAGRAPH	"Proper exercise is a major component of a good fitness program. Stretching exercises, for example, are a very effective means of reducing tension and improving flexibility. Such exercises include...."
SECOND PARAGRAPH	"The best way to burn calories and fat is through aerobic exercise...."
THIRD PARAGRAPH	"Finally, there are a number of exercises that help to strengthen and tone muscles...."

As you can see, subdividing the material this way keeps the paragraphs to a manageable length. Each paragraph is still clearly connected to the thesis.

Exercise

Choose one of the following topics:

1. the advantages of allowing stores and other businesses to remain open on Sundays
2. the disadvantages of allowing stores and other businesses to remain open on Sundays
3. the major stages in my life
4. the reasons that some people get into debt
5. fashions that are now "out" and fashions that are now "in"

Now follow these steps:

1. Decide on your purpose for writing: to explain, to share personal experience, to persuade.
2. Write your specific goal for the essay by completing this sentence: *My goal is to ____.*
3. Freewrite on your subject for ten minutes or until you have enough material for three broad categories.
4. Look over the material and divide the ideas into categories.
5. Decide on the most effective way of arranging the categories.
6. Write a thesis that makes a point about your subject. The thesis should suggest the sections of the essay, in the order in which they will be discussed.
7. Write topic sentences for middle paragraphs. Arrange the topic sentences in the order in which the middle paragraphs will appear in the essay.

The Conclusion

In a deductive essay a good concluding paragraph leads naturally from the body and gives the paper a sense of completeness. The conclusion shouldn't appear to be tacked on as an afterthought. A brief statement such as *In this essay I have discussed the components of a good fitness program* is too abrupt and mechanical. Instead, the conclusion should reinforce the thesis by showing the importance or the implications of the main points. An effective final paragraph for an essay on fitness might read as follows:

> Jonathan Swift once noted that people desire long life but do not desire the declining strength and infirmities of old age. Increasingly, weakness and ill health need not be the natural consequences of aging. While staying fit does not guarantee longevity and certainly cannot promise eternal youth, exercising regularly, eating well to stay well, and controlling stress in your life can contribute to a healthier, more rewarding old age. As exercise and nutrition buffs know, fitness can add years to your life and life to your years.

Patterns for Comparison Essays

The Block Method

The block method of comparison is best used in short comparison essays on familiar subjects. When you compare two people, places, things, or ideas using the block method, you discuss everything about one side before

[*Forms of Writing,* Part 3: 8c]

you discuss the other. If, for instance, you are writing a comparison essay evaluating two hockey players, you might formulate the following thesis:

> A consideration of the skating and stick-handling abilities of X and Y shows that Y is clearly the more experienced and polished player.

In the first half of the essay, you would analyze the skating and stick-handling of player X. In the second half you would discuss player Y, using the same points for comparison, namely skating and stick-handling.

The Alternating Method

The alternating method of comparison is better for longer, more complex comparisons. To use this method, decide on the basis for comparing your subjects. In one section of the essay, compare the subjects on one point, move on to another section comparing the subjects on a new point, and so on. Let's say that you want to develop a comparison essay on two hockey teams using this thesis:

> Team A has a better chance of making the play-offs this year than Team B because Team A has stronger offensive players, more experienced defensive players, and a greater commitment to teamwork and good sportsmanship.

In the body of the essay, you would discuss offensive players on both teams, then compare defensive players on both teams, and then analyze teamwork and sportsmanship in both teams. You would develop separate points of comparison in separate paragraphs.

Making the Essay Flow

In the section on paragraph development, we discussed the importance of showing how ideas within a paragraph are connected. In an essay it is also important to show how paragraphs are connected to each other. You can connect paragraphs by using transitional words and phrases and by repeating the key idea of one paragraph in the topic sentence for the next. The following model shows you how you can make these connections.

> THESIS: In order to excel, people need to develop the qualities of both their left brain and their right brain.

TOPIC SENTENCES:

MIDDLE PARAGRAPH #1	The left hemisphere of the brain specializes in logical thinking and in language.
MDDLE PARAGRAPH #2	While the left side of the brain specializes in linear, sequential thinking, the right side specializes in intuitive, creative thought.

As you read through the draft of an essay, check to see that each paragraph leads clearly into the next. Don't make your readers leap from section to section; use transitions to build effective bridges.

5
Practice in Writing Essays

A. Writing to Explain

[*Forms of Writing,* Part 3: 10c]

Writing Situation 5: The "How-To" Article

Your goal in the how-to article is to explain one of the following procedures:

1. how to plant a garden
2. how to improve a child's table manners
3. how to convince your parents to leave you (a teenager) the house and car keys for the weekend
4. how to train a dog or cat
5. a topic of your choice

Assume that you have been asked to write this how-to article for a magazine that caters to a specific type of reader, e.g., gardeners, parents, teens, pet owners. Suit the topic to the reader. If you choose to write on your own topic, decide on the kind of magazine in which your article will appear.

Your piece should be about 500 words in length. The amount of detail you include depends partly on the complexity of the procedure and partly on your reader's level of experience and knowledge. Remember that you are not writing a paragraph; you are writing a longer piece that will contain several paragraphs.

Preparing

1. Create an audience profile for the readers of your magazine. What is their level of expertise? What do they need and want to know?
2. Bearing your reader in mind, make a preliminary list of the steps in the procedure, in chronological order.

Drafting

1. Write a short introduction that encourages your reader by pointing out the usefulness of the procedure. Include information on any necessary tools and materials, and where to get them.
2. Describe the steps for your procedure in the order in which your reader will carry them out. Put each major step in a separate paragraph. Provide enough detail to explain each step clearly.
3. Write a short conclusion that makes your instructions sound finished and that reminds your reader why learning how to perform this procedure is worthwhile.

Revising

1. As you read over your work, ask yourself these questions:
   a) Are the directions complete? Have I listed all equipment or materials my reader might need at the beginning of my instructions? Is each step clear? Have I defined unfamiliar terms and anticipated possible problems?
   b) Is the sequence of steps clear?
   c) Are the steps given in parallel sentence structure? If you have listed equipment or materials, are all the items in the list grammatically parallel? (See the sections dealing with Parallelism in the workbook and the text.)
   d) Are most of the directions phrased as command/request sentences?

   Example: Be sure the thread matches the fabric.

   In these sentences, "you" is the understood subject.

2. Rewrite your article, making any necessary changes.
3. Proofread carefully. For help with particular problems in grammar, sentence structure, and punctuation, see the relevant sections of the workbook and the text.

Writing Situation 6: The Summary

A summary is a shortened version of a longer work. When you summarize, you pick out the main points and include only enough detail to make them clear. Summarizing is a useful skill because it forces you to understand the material you are working with and because it gives you practice explaining another writer's ideas in your own words.

For this assignment, choose a magazine article 4-5 pages long and summarize it.

Preparing

1. Look for an article that deals with concepts and ideas—an article in which a writer presents a thesis and develops it. Avoid news articles and accounts of personal experiences.
2. Read the whole article carefully.
3. Look for an introductory summary within the article (often this summary is located just below the title of the article). Check for obvious section divisions and headings. These will help you to get a sense of major divisions in the article.
4. Read the article again, this time circling key words and underlining topic sentences. These main idea sentences are often located at the beginning and/or the end of the paragraph.
5. Take notes on the article, section by section. Be sure to put the main ideas in your own words and to define any key terms.
6. Note the full title of the article, the name(s) of the author(s), the name of the magazine, the date, and the page numbers. For more information on noting sources, see *Forms of Writing*, Documentation (24c).

Drafting

1. Begin your summary with the main idea of the whole article. Be careful not to confuse the subject with the author's main point about that subject. The article, for example, might be about PCB's. The writer's main point might be that PCB's are less dangerous than is commonly supposed.
2. Include the title of the article and the author's name in the sentence stating the main idea of the article so that it's obvious you are writing a summary.

Example

Sabrina Asanti's point in "AIDS and the Yuppie" is that the fear of AIDS is making the upper middle class much more sexually conservative than it was twenty years ago.

3. Include enough detail from each section of the article to cover the main points. Be sure to include and define any key terms.

Revising

1. As you read over your summary, ask yourself these questions:
   a) Is this summary an accurate reflection of the original? Have I avoided over-emphasizing a point I found especially interesting? Have I avoided substituting my own ideas for those that the writer has expressed?
   b) Does my summary begin with the main idea of the whole article? Does it include only enough detail to make the development of that idea in the article clear?
   c) Have I included all the bibliographical information about the article either in the title of the summary or in the introduction?
   d) Is most of the summary in my own words? Have I put quotation marks around any quotation of more than three consecutive words?
2. Rewrite your summary, making any necessary changes.
3. Proofread carefully. Check the relevant sections of the workbook and the text for help with grammar, sentence structure, and punctuation.

Writing Situation 7: The Expository Essay

[*Forms of Writing*, Part 2: 5d-e; Part 3: 10a-b]

Causal analysis is one common method of developing an explanation. In a causal analysis, you may examine how a number of effects are the results of one cause or how a number of causes have contributed to a particular effect.

Suppose, for example, that you have been asked by the editor of a newsletter for parents of high school students to write a short piece (about 500 words) titled "Why Kids Run Away from Home." Running away from home is the effect. Your purpose is to explain the reasons why kids run away. Keep your approach objective and neutral, but be sure to include examples that will make the reasons for running away vivid for your readers.

Preparing

1. Begin by making a list of reasons under these two headings, which represent the two main categories of information in the essay:

   Reasons to Run *from* Home
   Reasons to Run *to* Somewhere Else

2. Prepare a brief profile of your audience. Ask yourself what parents need and want to know.
3. With the needs of your audience in mind, select the most important reasons in each of the main categories.
4. Flesh out some of these reasons with examples drawn from your own experience or imagination.
5. Decide how to organize the categories. Which will you discuss first—reasons to run *from* something or reasons to run *to* something more desirable? Within each category, put the reasons that most parents can identify with last.

Drafting

1. Write a thesis that makes a point about the subject and that suggests the categories in the order in which they will appear in the essay.
2. Write a topic sentence for your first middle paragraph. Develop this section with reasons and examples that will make the perspective of the kid who runs away clear to your readers. If you have more material than can easily be handled in one paragraph, divide the information into subsections.
3. Write a topic sentence for the middle paragraph(s) of the second category. Develop this section fully with clear, vivid details, again using more than one paragraph if necessary.
4. Go back to your thesis. Write several sentences for an introductory paragraph, with the thesis appearing at the end of this introduction. Write a concluding paragraph to reinforce your main point.

Revising

1. As you read over your draft, ask yourself these questions:
   a) Does my introduction capture my reader's interest? Is the point of my essay clear?
   b) Have I placed my most important category last? Within each category, have I arranged the ideas clearly and logically?
   c) Have I written effective topic sentences for my middle paragraphs? Does the body of each paragraph develop its main idea fully? Are the connections between ideas clear?
   d) Does my concluding paragraph give the essay a sense of completeness?
2. Rewrite your essay, making any necessary changes.
3. Proofread your work carefully. Pay particular attention to errors identified in other pieces of writing. If you need help, check the relevant sections in the workbook and the text.

B. Writing to Share Personal Experience

Writing Situation 8: The Personal Narrative Essay

[*Forms of Writing*, Part 3: 11a-b]

A **narrative** is essentially an account of events arranged in chronological sequence. In some kinds of writing, such as an anecdote, this sequence of events is enough. In an essay, however, you need to make a point about what the experience means to you. Thus it's not so much the experience (exciting as that may have been) but what you say about it that makes a good personal narrative essay. For this reason, even quite ordinary experiences—shopping for jeans, opening a bank account, studying for an exam—can provide good subjects for a personal narrative essay, provided that the experience has given you something worthwhile to think about and share with your reader.

Usually the point of a good personal narrative essay is something you learned about yourself or another person. Shopping for jeans, for instance, might have made you wonder why you have accepted without question the standards society sets for physical beauty. Opening a bank account might have fooled you into thinking you had taken the first step towards maturity. Studying for an exam might have revealed more inner resources than you knew you possessed.

To write effectively about an incident that gave you this sort of insight into yourself, or someone close to you, or even an institution (such as a school, bank, or government agency), you need to select the details that relate to your point about the incident's significance.

Write your account as a personal essay at least 500 words in length.

Preparing

1. Choose a single incident or event that changed your outlook. Such incidents might include hitting your first home run, getting into trouble, seeing your little brother go out for his first date.
2. To give yourself a clearer sense of what you want to say about this experience, complete this sentence:

_____ was important to me because

_____ .

Drafting

1. Write an account of this incident. Keep the details in chronological sequence unless you have a good reason for flashbacks.

[For more on inductive patterns, see *Forms of Writing*, Part 3: 8b]

2. Read over what you have written to see if a point about its significance to you emerges. State this point in a sentence or two. If you decide to organize your essay inductively (a common organizational pattern for this kind of essay), your main point should come at the end. If you decide to organize your work deductively, state your main point near the beginning.

Revising

1. As you read over your draft, ask yourself these questions:
   a) Have I made a clear point about the significance of this experience?
   b) Have I included enough detail to make my point convincing and my experience real?
   c) Have I maintained a clear chronological sequence?
   d) Is my material obviously organized in either an inductive or a deductive pattern?
2. Rewrite your essay, making any necessary changes.
3. Proofread your work carefully.

[*Forms of Writing*, Part 3: 11c-d]

Writing Situation 9: The Short Personal Descriptive Essay

What would your ideal house, car, boat, or vacation spot be like? Could you describe any one of these so that its especially appealing features are clear to your readers?

In **descriptive** writing you provide your readers with the details they need to imagine how something looks, sounds, feels, tastes, or moves. In **subjective description**, you try to convey the dominant impression these details make on you. Thus subjective description reveals as much about you as about the person, place, or object you are describing. Try to include a wide range of sensory details in your description, but be sure that all these details create a single dominant impression. The dominant impression of a bedroom, for instance, might be chaos or comfort, depending on the details you include.

For this assignment, write a short essay (about one page) describing your ideal anything.

Preparing

1. Write the name of the person, place, or object you are describing in the centre of the page. Then write all the words you can think of suggesting how it looks, feels, and sounds. Include words to describe taste and movement if these are appropriate.
2. Do these details suggest a dominant impression about your subject—relaxation? excitement? speed? security? power?
3. Freewrite for five minutes, focusing on the descriptive details that convey this dominant impression.

Drafting

1. Give yourself a clear sense of your specific goal by filling in the blanks in this sentence:

   The main impression I want to convey about my ideal _____ is _____.

2. Using the material from your freewriting exercise, write a draft of your essay.

Revising

1. As you read over your draft, ask yourself these questions:
   a) Have I provided enough information about my subject to make my description precise and real?
   b) Do all the details fit with the dominant impression I want to convey about this subject?
   c) Have I organized the details so that my reader can form a clear visual image of the object I am describing?
2. Rewrite your descriptive essay, making any necessary changes.
3. Proofread your work carefully. If you need help with grammar and sentence structure, see the relevant sections in the workbook and text.

Writing Situation 10: The Personal Reflective Essay

[Forms of Writing, Part 3: 11e-f]

The **personal reflective** essay, as its name suggests, gives you an opportunity to present your thoughts and feelings about a particular topic. The material in reflective essays is not usually organized chronologically (as it is in narrative essays). Instead, you are more likely to analyze causes and effects, to compare, perhaps even to define and evaluate, as you move back and forth between statements about what something means to you and the specific details you need to support those statements.

For this assignment, write a 500-word personal essay explaining how being away from home helped you to see your family in a new light. You might want to focus your essay on how you now see a particular person (a parent or sibling) differently or on how your perspective on the whole family has changed.

In either case, you will need to think carefully about your subject to formulate the point you want to make about it. A thesis such as *My feelings about my brother have certainly changed over the past five years* is not specific enough. A thesis such as *The black sheep of the family turned out to be a scapegoat* would provide a clearer focus for what you now understand about your brother—that he was more sinned against than sinning.

Remember that your thesis, whether implied or explicitly stated, will be more convincing to your reader if you provide plenty of specific details to support what you are saying.

If the suggested topic doesn't appeal to you, write about any situation that you now see from a new perspective—an illness, a job, a marriage, and so forth.

Preparing

1. To get started, spend five minutes freewriting on the subject "Living at Home" (Being Ill with _____, Working at _____, or Being Married to _____). Read over what you have written to see if a dominant impression, such as security or constriction, emerges. Try to express this impression in a sentence or two. If this freewriting strategy seems profitable, repeat it with "Leaving Home" (or a suitable variation on another topic).
2. Remember that the subject of this essay is how your perspective has changed. To work out a main point for your essay, complete this sentence:

   Leaving home gave me a new perspective on _____ because _____.

3. Make a list of the main points you want to cover in your essay. Be sure that all of them are connected to the change in your perspective.

Drafting

1. Keep your material focused on the reason for your change of attitude. Is this change the result of changes within you, changes in your subject, or changes in both?

2. Include details and relevant examples.
3. Try to organize your work inductively by beginning with specific details and gradually leading your reader to your thesis.

Revising

1. As you read over your work, ask yourself these questions:
   a) Does all the material make my own thoughts and feelings about this experience clear to my readers?
   b) Could I expand and clarify my thoughts and feelings through comparison, cause and effect analysis, definition, or evaluation? For more information on these methods of developing paragraphs, see the appropriate entries in *Forms of Writing*, Part 2: 5a-e; 6a-d.
2. Rewrite your work, making any necessary changes.
3. Proofread your work carefully. Pay particular attention to errors you habitually make (in the use of the apostrophe to show possession, for instance). For help, see the relevant sections of the workbook and the text.

Writing Situation 11: Comic Writing: Comparing Two Things

[*Forms of Writing*, Part 2: 6b; Part 3: 7a; 8c; 11]

Humour often arises from incongruity. This incongruity usually arises from the difference between what we expect and what we get. Sometimes the laugh is on the writer, who reveals the gap between expectation and reality in a personal experience. Sometimes the laugh is on the reader, who has been led to expect one thing and gets another. Comparison works well as a method of development in comic writing because it is organized around a presentation of similarities and differences.

As you are experimenting with both the content and the language of comic writing, remember that a certain degree of detachment is often a necessary ingredient of humour. Having a waiter dump spaghetti all over your best clothes on a first date is probably not funny at the time. You need to see this situation from a distance to appreciate the humour.

In this assignment, you will write a short comic essay (about 500 words) sharing a personal experience or personal reflections. Your method of development is comparison. Your subject can be any two things you can compare with a comic stance: boyfriends or girlfriends, cars, pets, houses, sports, or (as a way of emphasizing the comic) a boyfriend and a pet, a house and a car. If you find that you are emphasizing the features that make one better than the other, see Evaluation (6d) in *Forms of Writing* for more information on assessing strengths and weaknesses.

51

Preparing

1. Put the names of the two things you're comparing at the top of a sheet of paper. Then write the most important characteristics of each.
2. Group these characteristics into categories. You may find it easiest to explore the comic potential in your subjects by applying the categories that would normally be appropriate for one subject (such as appearance, cost, and performance for a car) to another (such as a pet or a girlfriend). Make sure you have parallel categories for the two things you are comparing.
3. Select the most important similarity or difference and use it as the basis of your comparison. Then decide what main point you want to make about the comparison. Make this main point the thesis of your essay.
4. Decide which pattern of development to use—the block method (where you say everything about A before you discuss B) or the alternating method (where you deal with one aspect of A and B in each paragraph).

Drafting

1. Write a sentence or two expressing your thesis.
2. Select the most important points from the list you made and write your draft. Be sure all the material in it is clearly connected to your thesis.

Revising

1. As you read over your work, ask yourself these questions:
   a) Have I made the basis of my comparison clear to my reader?
   b) Have I said enough about one subject before moving to the other? Remember that the "ping-pong" effect can be amusing in a single paragraph but becomes wearing in a whole essay.
   c) Have I used transitions to move my reader smoothly from point to point?
   d) Have I maintained a comic stance in both the content and the tone of my essay?
2. Rewrite your essay, making any necessary changes.
3. Proofread your work carefully. For help with specific problems, see the relevant sections of the workbook and the text.

C. Writing to Persuade

Writing Situation 12: Letter to the Editor

[*Forms of Writing,* Part 2: 6d; Part 3: 12d]

In this assignment you will write a **persuasive essay** that takes the form of a letter to the editor. You will establish the main point in the introduction and develop broad categories of information in separate paragraphs, as you would for an essay, but you will present your essay as a letter. For information on standard letter format, see the model in the following section on business letters. Address the letter to your local newspaper. You will find the name of the letters editor and the address on the letters page.

Your purpose in this letter is to persuade the readers of the newspaper that something is good or bad: the proposed tax increase is unnecessary; statutory holidays are more expensive than most people recognize; police officers should or should not have the right to strike. Choose a topic that interests you and write a letter of 250-300 words.

To be persuasive, you will need to decide whether your readers are likely to be friendly, hostile, or neutral, and you will need to be clear about your perspective for evaluation. Are you in favour of (or opposed to) your subject on moral grounds, on practical grounds, or both? Which perspective is more likely to convince your reader? Once you have answered these questions, you can choose appropriate persuasive strategies, such as appeals to authority, examples, prediction of consequences, and so forth.

[*Forms of Writing,* Part 3: 12a]

Preparing

1. Try to focus on a specific issue. Instead of writing about pollution, make a plea for people to recycle newspapers, bottles, and cans.
2. Make a brief profile of the readers of this newspaper. Are they likely to agree or disagree with your position on this issue? What kinds of arguments will appeal to them?
3. Decide whether you want to focus on moral arguments, practical arguments, or both.
4. List the strongest arguments for your position. Then list the most likely objections to it.

Drafting

Remember that newspaper columns are narrow, so your paragraphs should be short. One way to organize this letter would be to write four paragraphs covering the following:

1. The issue and your position on it. Are you writing as a spokesperson for a group? as a concerned citizen?
2. The most common objections and their validity.
3. Specific reasons to support your own position.
4. A practical solution to the problem.

Revising

1. As you read over your work, ask yourself these questions:
   a) Does the letter have all the parts of the business letter: return address, correspondent's address, salutation, complimentary closing, signature?
   b) Are both the issue and my position on it clear?
   c) Will my reasons for this position appeal to my readers?
   d) Do I present myself as a reasonable person talking to other reasonable people?
2. Rewrite your letter, making any necessary changes.
3. Proofread carefully. You don't want grammatical mistakes and spelling errors to undermine your credibility. For help, check the relevant sections of the workbook and the text.

[Forms of Writing, Part 2: 6d; Part 3: 12d]

Writing Situation 13: The Persuasive Letter

Suppose that you have been asked to represent a group of concerned parents, teachers, and students who want to persuade your local school board to establish a day care centre for high school students with children. Write a two-page letter to Ms. Francine Lalonde, chairperson of your local school board, explaining the need for this facility and arguing that it is the board's responsibility to provide it.

You will develop this assignment as you would a persuasive essay, but you will present it as a letter. See the model in the following section on business letters for standard letter format.

Preparing

1. Write a brief profile of Ms. Lalonde, emphasizing the main concerns of a person in her position.
2. List the problems currently caused by the absence of this facility in your high school.
3. List the benefits of having a day care centre that meets the needs of teen parents who want to complete high school.

4. Decide whether you want to focus your letter on moral arguments, practical arguments, or both.

Drafting

1. Begin by acknowledging the most obvious arguments against putting a day care centre in a high school.
2. Write a paragraph or two explaining the current problems caused by the absence of this facility. Give relevant examples where appropriate.
3. Write a paragraph or two explaining the benefits of creating a day care within your high school. Include the benefits to teen parents, other students, the reputation of the school and the school board. Emphasize the benefits that will appeal to the chairperson of the school board.

Revising

1. As you read over your letter, ask yourself these questions:
   a) Have I used standard letter format, including return address (which you can invent), correspondent's address, salutation, complimentary closing, signature?
   b) Do my methods of persuasion correspond with my reader profile? (You can assume that Ms. Lalonde is skeptical, but open-minded.)
   c) Have I established common ground with this reader by acknowledging opposing points of view?
   d) Have I sequenced my points so that my strongest arguments (practical, moral, or both) come last?
2. Rewrite your letter, making any necessary changes.
3. Proofread carefully. For information on specific points of grammar and sentence structure, see the relevant sections in the workbook and the text.

Writing Situation 14: The Review

Reviews provide evaluations of such things as rock concerts, restaurants, movies, and television programs. When you write a review, your purpose is to assess the strengths and weaknesses of your subject and to affect your readers' actions (Don't buy this book!) or to shape their attitudes and opinions (This television miniseries was definitely worth watching). The most useful perspectives for your evaluation are usually moral (Are the values portrayed good or bad?) and aesthetic (Is this a well-made thing of its kind?). Be sure to make your perspective (s) obvious to your reader.

[*Forms of Writing,* Part 2: 6d; Part 3: 12f-g]

For this assignment, assume that you are the arts critic for your local newspaper. Write a 500-word review of a movie you have seen recently or of a television series you have been watching fairly consistently. You will probably need to provide a brief summary of the most important features of your subject because your readers may not have seen the movie or television program you are reviewing. Be sure to include information on where and when it can be seen.

Preparing

1. If you are writing a movie review, there are several considerations you should keep in mind as you jot down notes for your draft. You need to give your readers some idea of what the movie is about (without giving away any surprise endings), but don't limit yourself to a plot summary. Show what thematic ideas lie behind the movie and what means the director uses to convey them. You might also consider the contribution of mood (or atmosphere), acting quality, and/or any special scenes that notably enhance or detract from the impact of the movie. Is this movie strong in technique but weak in theme and characterization? strong in both? weak in both?

2. If you review a television series, be insightful in similar sorts of ways. Try, for instance, to detect similarities in outlook and treatment from one episode to another. Point out formulas and stereotyping that may—or may not— affect the show's popularity. If you think that this is a superior series, try to show what makes it superior. Does it break from standard patterns in theme, characterization, and technique?

Drafting

1. Your introduction should convey your enthusiasm (or lack of it) and give your general opinion of the movie or television series.
2. Begin with a brief summary and then include specific examples of what you liked or disliked. Try to balance negatives and positives; remember that what appealed to you may not appeal to everyone. Be sure to include information about times, channels, theatres, dates as appropriate.
3. End with a snappy conclusion.

Revising

1. As you read over your work, ask yourself these questions:
   a) Have I included enough information to give my readers a sense of the movie or television series and to support either a positive or negative judgment?

b) Have I kept the focus on my subject rather than on my own reactions? Often you can maintain this focus by rephrasing. Instead of saying *I particularly liked the car chase,* say *The car chase was the most exciting part of the movie.*

c) Have I maintained a balanced perspective?

2. Rewrite your review, making any necessary changes.

3. Proofread carefully. See the relevant sections of the workbook and text for help with grammar, sentence structure, and punctuation.

Writing Situation 15: The Persuasive Essay

[*Forms of Writing,* Part 3: 12b; Revising 8]

Do you think the number of immigrants and refugees that Canada accepts each year should be increased or decreased? What criteria would you apply if you were setting immigration policy—language? racial origin? skills? educational background? financial resources? need for refuge? age? desire for a better economic future? family unification?

Imagine that you are presenting a 500-word newspaper editorial on Canadian immigration policy. Set out your position on whether immigration policy should be tightened or relaxed, and give your reasons for the criteria you think should be applied.

Preparing

1. Think over the possible cultural, economic, and moral implications of changing current immigration policy. Spend a few minutes brainstorming on this topic by completing these outlines:

Positive Effects of Admitting More Immigrants and Refugees

For Canada	For Prospective Immigrants
1.	1.
2.	2.
3.	3.

Negative Effects of Admitting More Immigrants and Refugees

For Canada	For Prospective Immigrants
1.	1.
2.	2.
3.	3.

2. Read over your outlines and decide whether you want to emphasize practical arguments, moral arguments, or both.
3. Decide which of these will be most convincing to the readers of this newspaper.

Drafting

1. Begin by stating your position.

   Canada should tighten/relax current immigration policy because

   _____ .

2. Establish common ground with readers who hold a different position by briefly summarizing the opposing arguments and acknowledging their validity where you can.
3. Present reasons to support your position.

Revising

1. As you read over your work, ask yourself these questions:
   a) Are my arguments logically consistent with the emphasis I want to place on practical and/or moral standards of evaluation?
   c) Does the argument with the most appeal to my readers come last?
2. Rewrite your paper, making any necessary changes .
3. Proofread carefully. Pay particular attention to the errors you know you're most likely to make (in subject-verb agreement or faulty parallelism, for instance). Check the relevant sections of the workbook and text for help.

6
Business Letters and Reports

Business Letters

With the ready availability of telephones, fewer people are writing letters to family and friends. However, letters are still a very important means of business communication. You may write letters to apply for a job, to express your dissatisfaction with a company's service, or to make a request of someone. Because you want your reader to take your application, complaint, or request seriously, your letter should be accurate, complete, clear, and business-like. To make your writing clear and business-like, try these techniques:

[*Forms of Writing*, Part 4: 14]

1. Keep sentences and paragraphs fairly short.
2. Avoid long-winded expressions such as *Please be advised that* or *Enclosed please find for your perusal*.
3. Use standard letter format, as in this model:

123 Main Street
Brandon, Manitoba   [return address, single-spaced,
R7A 6V8   including the current date]
July 1, 19xx

Ms. Louise Santiago, Manager
High-Tech Computer Applications   [the address of the person or the
9876 Portage Avenue   organization to whom you are
Winnipeg, Manitoba   writing, single-spaced]
R3J 1P3

Dear Ms. Santiago: [the greeting, followed by a colon]

THE BODY OF THE LETTER
[usually no more than one page]

Yours truly,   [the closing, followed by a comma]

                                                  [your signature]

Enclosure: [if there are any enclosures, such as a cheque or a résumé]
cc: [if copies of the letter are being forwarded to other people]

You will find a more detailed explanation of business letter features and format in *Forms of Writing*, Part 4, Business Letters (14).

Reports

Reports can range from informal memorandums to more formal pieces such as field reports and proposals. All reports are based on factual information. Some provide an interpretation of the data and recommendations or solutions to problems. The content and the format will depend on your purpose and on your reader's needs. Here, for example, is the standard format for a memorandum, the usual form of communication from one department to another in the same organization:

TO: Ellsworth Fitzhugh,   [the name and position of the
Managing Director   person to whom you are writing]

FROM: Cameron Carson, Office
Manager   [your name and position]

DATE: Sept. 7, 19xx   [the date on which you write the
                                    memorandum]

SUBJECT: Missing Office Supplies   [a precise statement of the main
                                    focus of the message]

THE BODY OF THE MEMORANDUM

                                    [your signature, underlined]
Cameron Carson   [your name typed below your
                                    signature]

The formats for a variety of reports are discussed in detail in *Forms of Writing*, Part 4: Reports (16); Proposals (17). Whatever format you use, your report should be accurate, concise, and complete.

7
Practice in Writing Letters and Reports

A. Writing to Explain

Writing Situation 16: Field Report in Memorandum Format

For this assignment, assume that you are reporting on an accident that has occurred in your workplace. Your audience is your supervisor. Write a memorandum to him or her, giving background information, analyzing the causes of the accident, and making recommendations to prevent such an accident from recurring.

[*Forms of Writing*, Part 4: Memorandums, 16d-e; Field Reports, 16g]

Preparing

1. Decide on your subject—either a specific accident or a type of accident.
2. Write a brief profile of your reader. What does a person in this position need and want to know?
3. Jot down the background information needed to give your reader a sense of context. Include the **who, what, when, where,** and **how** of the accident.
4. Make a list of the causes of this accident. Decide whether they are independent or interdependent. See *Forms of Writing*, Part 2: 5e (Causal Analysis) for more information.
5. Make a list of recommendations. Decide which ones are most important (no more than three) and make suggestions about how to implement them, if appropriate.

61

Drafting

Write a paragraph for each of the three main sections of your report: background, analysis, and recommendations.

Revising

1. As you read over your work, ask yourself these questions:
    a) Does this report follow the format required for a memorandum? Be especially careful to check the headings: TO, FROM, SUBJECT, DATE. End the memo with your signature.
    b) Have I included all the necessary information in the background section? Check what you have written against your reader profile.
    c) Does my analysis section focus on the causes of the accident? If the causes of this accident are independent of each other, have I sequenced them from most to least important? If the causes are interdependent, have I included transitions to make the cause and effect connections clear?
    d) Do my recommendations follow logically from the background and analysis sections of the report? Have I indicated which of my recommendations is the most important? Have I included suggestions on implementation, if appropriate?
2. Rewrite your work, making any necessary changes.
3. Proofread your work carefully. Check the relevant sections of the workbook and the text for help with specific problems.

[Forms of Writing, Part 4: 16i]

Writing Situation 17: The Problem-Solving Report

A problem-solving report describes a problem, provides an analysis of the causes and effects of the problem, and offers solutions.

To get a sense of the context in which a problem-solving report would be appropriate, assume that you are a volunteer worker in a youth shelter. One of the recurrent problems is that volunteer workers are seldom able to attend client conferences held by the centre's professional staff because these meetings are usually held during regular business hours. You are submitting a report (about two pages long) explaining the difficulties that arise as a result of this situation and recommending solutions. Your report, written on behalf of all volunteer workers, will be submitted to the director of the centre.

You can use this problem as the subject of your problem-solving report, but if you find this topic difficult, choose any local problem. Possible topics might be long lineups in the cafeteria during the lunch break, a high number of traffic accidents at a busy intersection, or a problem in management-staff relations. Your report should be addressed to a particular reader.

Preparing

Identify your reader. What would a person in his or her position need to know?

Drafting

Set up the report using standard memorandum format. The material in the body of the report will contain the following sections:

1. Background Section.
2. Analysis Section. Explain what you see as the causes and effects of this problem.
3. Recommendations Section. Make two or three specific recommendations that address the causes and/or the effects set out above.

Revising

1. As you read over your work, ask yourself these questions:
   a) Have I used the appropriate format?
   b) Have I included all the information that a person in the position of my reader would need to know?
   c) Do the recommendations follow logically from the background and analysis sections of the report? Is important information missing from either of these sections?
   d) Is the language in this report neutral and objective?
   e) Is the writing concise?
2. Rewrite your report, making any necessary changes.
3. Proofread carefully. Check the relevant sections of the workbook and the text for help with particular problems.

Writing Situation 18: Writing a Letter to Explain How Something Works

What invention would make the world a better place? Suppose you have come up with an invention that would do just that. In order to apply for a patent, you need to describe what your invention looks like and how it works. Depending on your invention, you may find that you can explain it best by showing how all the parts work together to produce the desired effect. Or you may find that you can explain your invention more satisfactorily by describing what it does in a step-by-step sequence.

Write a letter to Mr. Conrad Beamish, Director of Patent Application Reviews, describing your invention. You can find the address for your district patent office in the blue pages of your telephone book under Government of Canada, Consumer and Corporate Affairs Canada, Patents-Invention-Trademarks. You can make up the postal code or get the real one from the postal code directory at any post office. If there is no such office in your area, make up the address for one.

Preparing

1. Make a list of possible inventions. Some possibilities: a device that would clean up oil spills, or find socks that disappear mysteriously in the wash, or convert folding money instantly into change, or make kitty litter self-destruct. Use your imagination to think of others.
2. Try to visualize your invention. Consider size, weight, colour, need for power source, and so on.

Drafting

1. Explain the purpose of your invention by completing the following sentence:

   I am applying for a patent for _____, which is designed to _____.
2. Describe each of its parts and explain how they work together or explain what your invention does.

Revising

1. Your purpose here is to describe your invention, not to convince your reader of its worth. As you read over your work, ask yourself these questions:

a) Have I used standard letter format?

b) Is my descriptive language precise and objective? Have I focused on facts? For more information on objective description, see Description (5b) in *Forms of Writing*, Part 2.

c) Have I provided enough information about the components of this invention?

d) Have I made clear how these components work together to create their effect?

2. Rewrite your letter, making any necessary changes.

3. Proofread your work carefully. For help with problems in grammar and sentence structure, check the relevant sections of the workbook and text.

B. Writing to Persuade

Writing Situation 19: Letter of Complaint

[*Forms of Writing*, Part 4: 14c-d]

Most of us have felt from time to time that we would like to write a letter complaining about something—poor restaurant service, problems getting a car fixed or a compact disk player repaired, or delays in student loans, for example. Use one of these situations, or another that you've experienced, and write a one-page letter of complaint.

Preparing

1. Begin by identifying your reader and writing a brief profile that includes the information a person in his or her position—manager, owner, student loans officer—would need and want to know.

2. Collect all the information your reader needs.

3. Make up an address for your reader. Include his or her name and title, the name of the organization, and the street address, city, province and postal code.

Drafting

Letters of complaint usually include three short paragraphs:

1. A paragraph that explains the situation you are complaining about. Be sure to provide all the factual information your reader would need.

2. A paragraph explaining what you want done.

3. A paragraph expressing appreciation for your reader's attention.

Revising

1. As you read over your letter, ask yourself these questions:
   a) Does the letter have all the parts of the business letter: return address, correspondent's address, salutation, complimentary closing, signature?
   b) Are all of the middle paragraphs concise and complete? Check what you have written against your audience profile.
   c) Is the tone both friendly and businesslike?
2. Rewrite your letter, making any necessary changes.
3. Proofread your work carefully. A few slips in spelling, grammar, and punctuation may seriously undermine your credibility. Check the relevant sections of the workbook and text for help with specific problems.

[Forms of Writing, Part 4: 14g-h]

Writing Situation 20: Letter of Application

Imagine that you are writing a job application letter for a favourite television character. Alf, Olivia (from *Street Legal*), Data (from *Star Trek: the Next Generation*), and Klinger (from *M*A*S*H**) spring to mind as possibilities, but feel free to substitute your own choice.

Write a one-page letter of application for your character. Because you are pretending to be that person, you will describe your qualifications in the first person. If you were Alf, you might say, *My experiences as an alien have given me a unique perspective on the advertising industry.*

Preparing

1. Write a job description for your candidate—one that would appeal to your character and emphasize his or her strengths.
2. Write a brief reader profile for the person to whom your character would apply for this job. Make up a name, title, and place of business for your reader.
3. Make up an address for your reader, including street address and city, province, and postal code.

Drafting

Write a letter of application consisting of three paragraphs. Be sure to include:

1. the position applied for and the source of information about that position (newspaper ad, job posting, reference from a current employer)

2. the strengths and abilities that make you (as the television character) the ideal candidate
3. an expression of appreciation, and information about where your character can be reached for an interview.

Revising

1. As you read over your letter, ask yourself these questions:
   a) Does the letter match the job description and reader profile? Have I included all the information needed to "sell" my character?
   b) Does the letter have all the parts of a business letter: writer's address, correspondent's address, salutation, complimentary closing, and signature?
   c) Is the tone both friendly and businesslike?
2. Rewrite your letter, making any necessary changes.
3. Proofread your letter very carefully. A few mistakes could ruin your candidate's chances for a new career. Check the relevant sections of the workbook and text if you need more information.

PART 2

PRACTICE WITH SENTENCE STRUCTURE, GRAMMAR, AND PUNCTUATION

8

Sentence Structure

Correcting Sentence Fragments

Problem

A **fragment** is a grammatically incomplete construction. It may be a **phrase,** lacking a subject, a verb, or both a subject and a verb:

> PHRASE   A great day for our team.

Or it may be a **subordinate clause:**

> SUBORDINATE CLAUSE   Because it was a great day for our team.

In some situations, you can use a fragment effectively for emphasis, provided that most of your sentences are grammatically complete. To use an intentional fragment for emphasis, you need to eliminate unintentional fragments from your writing.

Fragments will make your writing seem less formal, however. It is therefore a good idea to avoid fragments in business writing and formal essays. Even in more informal writing, use fragments sparingly.

Basic Rule

To be grammatically complete, every sentence must contain at least one **main clause.**

A clause contains a **subject** and a **verb.** The verb may be a single word (*walk*) or a verb phrase (*has been walking*). Remember that a participle (*walking*) does not function as a verb unless it has an auxiliary. (See Recognizing Auxiliary Verbs in the Grammar section of this workbook for more information.)

71

FRAGMENT	The man walking down the aisle.
COMPLETE	The man is walking down the aisle.

A **main clause** can stand on its own:

I want to talk with you about your proposal.

A **subordinate clause** is introduced with a subordinate conjunction and cannot stand on its own as an independent sentence:

Because I want to talk with you about your proposal.

Note: Don't be misled by length. A complete sentence can be short: *I am ready.* A fragment can be long: *Whenever he heard the ringing bell, which recalled to him the championship days of his prize-fighting career.*

Exercise 1: Recognizing Fragments

Label each complete sentence *S* and each fragment *F*.

1. The carpet, once vibrant with colour, being now faded and worn.
2. The twin stars Castor and Pollux form the constellation Gemini.
3. Because no one made any effort to help.
4. Who knows the murderer's identity?
5. The detective, who is the only person who knows the murderer's identity.
6. He looked at his watch.
7. And saw that it was too late to change his plans.
8. McNamara, the leader of the band, a fine musician and a talented conductor.
9. Call me tomorrow.
10. If you get a chance.

Revision Strategies

1. Add a subject, a verb, or both to a phrase.

FRAGMENT	One last thing to do.
COMPLETE	I have one last thing to do.

2. Remove the subordinate conjunction introducing a subordinate clause, or add a main clause to a subordinate clause.

FRAGMENT	Although the movie doesn't start until midnight.
COMPLETE	The movie doesn't start until midnight.
COMPLETE	Although the movie doesn't start until midnight, we have decided to go.

3. Sometimes a fragment has been separated from the sentence of which it is actually a part. To correct this error, reattach the fragment to the sentence, using a comma or other punctuation if required.

FRAGMENT   Some people love escargots. Whereas others become squeamish at even the thought of eating snails.

COMPLETE   Some people love escargots, whereas others become squeamish at even the thought of eating snails.

Exercise 2: Correcting Fragments

Correct the following sentence fragments.

1. The townspeople waited nervously for the results of the lottery. Knowing the winner's fate.

_____

2. He has one ambition in life. To travel the world over, seeking fame and fortune.

_____

3. Hoping to hear from you soon. I remain your humble servant.

_____

4. Caroline won the race. Even though she had a broken bone in her foot.

_____

5. Rushing out the door, racing down the street, and shouting wildly at the bus disappearing in a fog of exhaust fumes.

_____

Exercise 3: Correcting Fragments

Revise the following paragraphs to eliminate sentence fragments.

1. The overcast sky blended with the grey of the land. The horizon appearing to be a confusing smudge of buildings, clouds, haze, and dirty snow. Smoke from metal chimneys drifted aimlessly over the city. Mixing with the new flakes that had begun to fall. The streets were a thick stew of decaying snow, salt, and sand. Which was churned by the heavy wheels of cars labouring to reach home before an early dusk.

2. Some people regard physical fitness as a means to physical health and well-being. Believing that vigorous exercise strengthens the heart and lengthens life. Other people exercise to make themselves more physically attractive. To reshape their bodies to fit the model that society presently holds as representative of physical perfection. Still others are more interested in exercise clothes than in exercise itself. They wear the latest fashions in running shoes, jogging suits, and headbands. But would never deign to work out for fear that sweat would ruin such expensive gear. Whatever the incentive, people want to be, or want to appear to be, part of the fitness scene. The demand for specialized clothing, equipment, books, video tapes, and memberships in fitness clubs having made exercise a profitable business.

Correcting Comma Faults

Problem

A **comma fault** occurs when two main clauses have been joined with only a comma:

> You bring the pizza, I'll bring my appetite.

Revision Strategies

1. Separate the two clauses with a period.

> You bring the pizza. I'll bring my appetite.

2. Add a **subordinate conjunction** (*because, although, if, unless, before, after, since, while*) to one of the clauses. If the subordinate clause comes first, put a comma after it.

> If you bring the pizza, I'll bring my appetite.

3. Add a **coordinate conjunction** (*and, but, or, nor, for, yet, so*) after the comma.

> You bring the pizza, and I'll bring my appetite.

Note: When the clauses are short, you can omit the comma.

4. If the clauses are closely related, you can replace the comma with a semicolon.

> You bring the pizza; I'll bring my appetite.

5. Replace the comma with a semicolon and a conjunctive adverb.

> You bring the pizza; then I'll bring my appetite.

Conjunctive adverbs include:

Cause & Effect	Contrast	Time Sequence	Addition
therefore	however	afterwards	furthermore
as a result	nevertheless	later	besides
consequently	otherwise	meanwhile	moreover
thus	instead	soon	in addition
		next	
		then	
		finally	

Note 1: Be sure to use a semicolon rather than a comma when any of these words is used as a conjunctive adverb to join two clauses.

NOT   Murray has been awarded a bursary, otherwise he would not be able to attend college.

BUT   Murray has been awarded a bursary; otherwise, he would not be able to attend college.

Note 2: Use a comma after a conjunctive adverb of more than two syllables: not after *thus*, but after *consequently*.

Murray was awarded a bursary; thus he could attend college.
Murray was awarded a bursary; consequently, he could attend college.

Note 3: Remember that words such as *however*, *therefore*, and *nevertheless* are sometimes used as parenthetical expressions rather than as conjunctive adverbs.

They agreed, therefore, to adjourn the meeting.

Notice that *therefore* is enclosed in commas.

Exercise 1

Correct each comma fault using one of the methods described above. Put C beside a correct sentence.

1. She was very nervous during the audition, as a result her voice cracked several times.

   _____

2. The library books were three months overdue, consequently Marla had to pay a substantial fine.

   _____

75

3. At one o'clock we were still waiting for our friends to join us for lunch, we decided to order without them.

_____

4. If I can manage to get some work done tonight, I can probably finish my essay.

_____

5. The driveway is being framed today, the workers will pour the concrete next week.

_____

6. The movie drags a bit in some places, but on the whole, I found it entertaining.

_____

7. Your application was submitted after the deadline, therefore, we cannot consider you for admission this term.

_____

8. Luigi was trying to call Gino at the office, Gino meanwhile was on a plane to Vancouver.

_____

9. "Friends, Romans, countrymen, lend me your ears, I come to bury Caesar, not to praise him."

_____

10. Please lend me the money for a hamburger, I promise to repay you on Tuesday.

_____

Exercise 2

Revise the following paragraphs to eliminate comma faults.

I planted my garden over the Victoria Day weekend, that was three days ago. Every day I peer intently at the ground, expecting carrots and peas to sprout and grow to maturity before my eyes. So far, there is not so much as a speck of green, the seeds remain only promises. I have put a great deal of effort into this endeavour, digging, hoeing, raking, planting each seed by hand in beautifully even rows. The vegetables should show some gratitude, at least, for my labours, they might even show a little initiative of their own and make the effort to sprout.

Why are they so reluctant to face life? I promise to take care of them, to water and fertilize them, to cut to the heart any weed and crush to oblivion any insect that threatens their comfort and security. They will not have to fear disease, they will not have to fear devouring slugs. I will help them to grow strong and healthy, to reach vegetable perfection, that is the least I can do. And when the time comes, they will enjoy a place of honour at my table. That also is the least I can do.

Correcting Fused Sentences

Problem

A **fused sentence,** sometimes called a run-on sentence, occurs when two sentences are written as one, with no punctuation between them:

> Please don't interrupt me I'm busy.
> The Gilberts live in the next apartment they fight every night.

Basic Rule

A **simple sentence** consists of one main clause.

> The stores were jammed with people.

A **compound sentence** consists of two main clauses joined by a comma and a coordinate conjunction, a semicolon, or a semicolon and a conjunctive adverb.

> The stores were jammed with people, for it was the last shopping day before Christmas.
> The stores were jammed with people; it was the last shopping day before Christmas.
> It was the last shopping day before Christmas; therefore, the stores were jammed with people.

To avoid fused sentences, the basic principle to keep in mind is that you need to signal the boundary between two main clauses.

Revision Strategies

1. Separate the two clauses with a period.
2. If the clauses are closely related, join them with a semicolon.

3. Join the two clauses with a comma and a coordinate conjunction (*and, but, or, nor, for, yet, so*).

> Please don't interrupt me, **for** I'm busy.

4. Join the two clauses with a semicolon and a conjunctive adverb such as *therefore, however, moreover, nevertheless, furthermore*.

> I'm busy; **therefore**, please don't interrupt me.

5. Turn one of the main clauses into a subordinate clause by adding a subordinate conjunction such as *because, although, since*, or into a relative clause by adding a relative pronoun such as *who, which*, or *that*. (See Practicing Subordination for more information.)

> **Because** I'm busy, please don't interrupt me.
> The Gilberts, **who** live in the next apartment, fight every night.

Exercise 1: Correcting Fused Sentences

Correct each fused sentence. Write C beside every correct sentence.

1. Victoria was queen of Great Britain from 1837 to 1901 after she died, she was succeeded by her son Albert Edward, who became King Edward VII.
2. The young child wore his mittens attached at either end of a long string that went around his neck.
3. The Sphinx challenged every passerby she demanded to know what walks on four legs in the morning, two in the afternoon, and three in the evening.
4. The monster destroyed those who could not provide an answer.
5. Oedipus, returning to Thebes, answered the riddle the Sphinx then killed herself.
6. Dodos were found on the island of Mauritius in the Indian Ocean the birds are now extinct.
7. Huge flocks of passenger pigeons once filled the skies of North America however, these birds are now extinct.
8. Adrian enjoyed wearing his brightly patterned shirt while on vacation in Hawaii, but he relegated it to the closet when he returned home to Guelph.
9. The severe thunderstorm has downed the power lines and disrupted service we'll be having cold cuts and salad for supper.
10. By the way, the answer to the Sphinx's riddle is man he crawls on all fours as a baby, walks upright on two legs in his prime, and uses a cane when he is old.

Exercise 2: Correcting Fused Sentences

Revise the following paragraph to correct fused sentences.

Children now in public school will likely face several career changes in their adult lifetime. Technological developments will make some jobs obsolete economic changes will result in decreased demands for certain professions and increased demands for others. It is understandable that a person who has spent several years at a community college, technical institute, or university will want to work in the field for which he or she has been trained. These days, however, fewer members of any graduating class are finding employment in their specific fields unemployment becomes a very real prospect. Graduates must therefore be flexible they must be able to transfer acquired skills to new fields and be willing to learn new skills when needed. Being able to think creatively, read efficiently, and communicate effectively is an integral part of this process.

Review Exercise 1: Fragments, Comma Faults, Fused Sentences

Correct any fragments, comma faults, or fused sentences. Put C beside a correct sentence.

1. Every weekend for several years Ramona and Jason and their friends played fantasy games. Like *Sword and Sorcery* and *Dungeons and Dragons*.

---

2. At first each adventure was new and exciting, eventually all the adventures seemed the same.

---

3. Jason and Ramona liked the friends they had made and didn't want to lose them.

---

4. Finally, one Saturday during summer vacation, Ramona suggested other activities. Cycling on a country road, exploring the ravine, and canoeing on the river.

---

5. Jason was enthusiastic the others weren't.

_____

6. They preferred the world of magic spells, imaginary combat, and hidden treasures.

_____

7. Disappointed, Ramona decided she would have to make some new friends, then she had an idea.

_____

8. She planned a fantasy adventure that would take them to a mysterious cave in the riverbank several kilometres away. While Jack collected costumes and made cardboard swords and daggers.

_____

9. The others were reluctant at first they soon changed their minds.

_____

10. There was buried treasure in the cave, if their quest was successful, they would find it.

_____

Correcting Dangling Modifiers

Problem

When a modifying phrase is not logically connected to any other part of a sentence, it is called a **dangling modifier**. The results can be confusing.

> After waiting several minutes for assistance, the clerk walked right past me and helped someone who had just come into the store.

An introductory phrase should modify the closest noun or pronoun in the sentence. The problem with this sentence is that *After waiting several minutes for assistance* seems to modify *clerk*.

After waiting several minutes for assistance is actually a reduced form of the clause *After I had waited several minutes for assistance*. Because the unexpressed subject of the phrase (*I*) is different from the subject of the main clause (*the clerk*), the phrase is left with nothing to modify.

Dangling modifiers do not occur in sentences where the unexpressed subject of the introductory phrase is the same as the subject of the main clause.

> After hunting everywhere (i.e., after **I** had hunted everywhere), **I** finally found my car keys in the garbage.

Note: Don't confuse dangling modifiers with **absolute phrases**. Absolute phrases do not dangle because they modify the whole sentence, as in these examples:

> **Given the amount of work we have to do,** I suggest that we start immediately.
> **All things considered,** Tom is the best person for the job.
> **Considering our state of confusion,** asking directions was the best thing to do.

Basic Rule

In order to act as a modifier, a phrase must logically describe some noun or pronoun in the sentence.

Revision Strategy

Expand the introductory phrase to a clause. If necessary, add the same subject to the main clause.

NOT	After starting to read the novel, it was difficult to put down.
BUT	After I had started to read the novel, I found it difficult to put down.

Exercise

Revise every sentence that contains a dangling modifier. Write *C* beside a correct sentence.

1. Realizing that my airline tickets were still on the coffee table, the taxi turned around and raced back to the apartment.

   _____

2. After washing with this beauty soap for seven days, my skin feels soft and smooth.

   _____

3. As a child, model boats were Walter's favourite toys.

   _____

4. According to Irish and Scottish folklore, the banshee's wail is a portent of death.

_____

5. Bored by the endless football games on television, reading a collection of medieval plays was a stimulating change.

_____

6. By exercising regularly, strength and endurance will improve.

_____

7. Waiting for the car dealership to open, there were several new models to look at.

_____

8. Standing out of the sun, the air is chilly.

_____

9. After walking out of the exam room, Bernie realized that he had forgotten to answer the questions on the last page.

_____

10. Exhausted by the steep incline, the top of the hill seemed to be getting farther away.

_____

11. When still an infant, Lorna's parents immigrated to Canada from Scotland.

_____

12. Placing the saucer on the floor, the thirsty kitten almost fell into the milk.

_____

13. Having worked at the same job for thirty-five years, Mrs. Leblanc looked forward to her retirement.

_____

14. After smoking one cigarette, carbon dioxide stays in the blood for six hours.

_____

15. After phoning her several times to set up an appointment, a place and time to meet were finally agreed upon.

_____

Correcting Misplaced Modifiers

Problem

A modifier is misplaced when it appears to modify a word it can't sensibly modify. Misplaced modifiers can be words, phrases, and subordinate clauses.

MISPLACED WORD	George had **almost** eaten the entire cake before he remembered that it was intended for the bake sale.
MISPLACED PHRASE	There is a picture of Grandfather during the First World War **on the dresser**.
MISPLACED CLAUSE	We attended a production at the Arden Theatre while visiting St. Albert, **which is part of the St. Albert Place complex**.

Basic Rule

A modifying word, phrase, or clause should be as close as possible to the construction it describes.

Revision Strategies

1. Be especially careful with words such as *almost, only, hardly, barely*, and *nearly*. These words are often misplaced.

   George ate **almost** the entire cake.

2. Be sure to put a prepositional or participial phrase close to the noun it modifies.

   There is a picture **on the dresser** of Grandfather during the First World War.

3. Be careful to put a clause introduced with *who, which*, or *that* close to the noun it modifies.

   While visiting St. Albert, we attended a production at the **Arden Theatre, which is** part of the St. Albert Place complex.

Exercise

Correct every sentence that contains a misplaced modifier. Write C beside a correct sentence.

1. Recently I read an article about a two-headed calf in the newspaper.
2. Alvin has almost dug the entire garden.

3. The Manchurian elm tree was toppled by a severe wind storm in the front yard.
4. The man was ejected from the room disrupting the meeting.
5. The patient described his out-of-body experience to the doctors lying on the bed.
6. For years regarded as loathsome relics of medical quackery, doctors are now using leeches to relieve blood congestion in grafted tissue such as reattached fingers.
7. Mr. and Mrs. Chau saw whales breaching close to shore while vacationing on Maui.
8. John has nearly seen every horror movie made since 1950.
9. Mrs. Semchuk was horrified to learn that her son Greg regularly eats cold pizza for breakfast.
10. The money was deposited in the bank representing the net proceeds from the sale of the house.
11. In one experiment, a chimpanzee typed the message that he had seen a snake in the woods using a portable computer keyboard with special symbols.
12. We attended a Sunday afternoon performance in the newly renovated dinner theatre.
13. After the fire, Helen was only left with the clothes she was wearing.
14. There is barely enough time to shower and change after gym class.
15. Rajiv was no closer to knowing how to fit the caramel into the chocolate bar after months of intensive research.

Review Exercise 2: Dangling and Misplaced Modifiers

Correct all dangling and misplaced modifiers. Put C beside a correct sentence.

1. At an early age, a second language is easily learned by most children.
2. By mimicking the sounds of the language, the pronunciation of German or Chinese or English words becomes part of the children's repertoire.
3. They only rely on what they hear, not on what they see in a book.
4. Thus children rapidly become very proficient in a second language.
5. As an adult, a second language is harder for me to learn.
6. Adults have more trouble with pronunciation taking a language course.
7. Before seeing the written words, for example, I may pronounce them correctly.
8. After seeing the words on the page, however, the sounds of the first language are transferred to the second.
9. My instructor nearly spends all the class time correcting these mistakes.
10. Before reading *"Auf Wiedersehen!"* it seems a good idea to let a child say it first.

Practicing Coordination

Principle

The basic principle of **coordination**, as its name suggests, is matching. When you coordinate your shirt with your pants, for example, you make sure that the colours, fabrics, and styles go together. You can do exactly the same thing with words, phrases, and clauses in a sentence. Coordination tells your reader that you consider the elements you are joining equally important.

Basic Rules

1. Use **coordinate conjunctions** (*and, but, or, nor, for, yet, so*) and **correlative conjunctions** (*either/or, neither/nor, not only/but also, both/and*) to join words, phrases and clauses to which you want to give equal emphasis.
2. Choose the most appropriate conjunction.
3. Make sure that these words, phrases, and clauses are grammatically parallel. For more information on how to do this, see Practicing Parallelism.

   You can see these stylistic devices at work in the following examples:

   > exhausted but triumphant [parallel adjectives]
   > neither a borrower nor a lender [parallel nouns]
   > out of the frying pan and into the fire [parallel prepositional phrases]
   > He wrote to her, but she did not reply. [parallel main clauses]

Exercise

Choose an appropriate conjunction to join words, phrases, and clauses in the following sentences.

1. My best friend is intelligent, sympathetic, _____ strong.
2. I think we should take the bus to the ski resort, _____ Alexander thinks we should take the car.
3. Your missing sweater is probably _____ lying on the picnic table _____ hanging in the hall closet.
4. Alice needed to borrow money for the down payment, _____ she made an appointment with the bank manager.
5. I have _____ the time _____ the inclination to do much research.

Correcting Faulty Coordination

Problem 1: Using the Wrong Conjunction

One source of faulty coordination involves using the wrong conjunction to join ideas:

> The article was well written but very informative.

Revision Strategies

1. Don't use *but* and *and* as if they were interchangeable. *But* signals a contrast in ideas. Since both comments about the article are positive, *but* doesn't make much sense. A more logical version of this sentence would replace *but* with *and*.

   > The article was well written **and** very informative.

2. Don't use *and* as an all-purpose conjunction. Use *and* when you want to show that what follows is an additional fact or idea. Use *but* and *yet* to express contrast, *for* and *so* to express cause and effect, and *or* and *nor* to express alternatives.

   NOT   Linda is saving money, and she wants to visit her parents in Hong Kong.

   BUT   Linda is saving money, for she wants to visit her parents in Hong Kong.
   or
   Linda wants to visit her parents in Hong Kong, so she is saving money.

Problem 2: Coordinating Unrelated Ideas

Coordinate conjunctions are inappropriate when the ideas joined have no obvious logical relationship with each other:

> The car has a silver metallic finish, and it gets excellent mileage both in the city and on the highway.

Revision Strategy

Express separate ideas in separate sentences.

> The car has a silver metallic finish. It gets excellent mileage both in the city and on the highway.

Problem 3: Coordinating Unequal Ideas.

A series of short simple sentences suggests that the sentences all express ideas of equal importance, even when they don't:

> Allison moved to Waterloo. It was 1988. She enrolled in the faculty of engineering. She was studying at the university.

Sometimes such a series can be effective, but overuse results in a choppy, immature style.

Revision Strategies

1. Combine short sentences in longer sentences. Put the main idea in the main clause and put less important ideas in subordinate clauses.

   > When Allison moved to Waterloo in 1988, she enrolled in the faculty of engineering at the university.

2. Sometimes you can revise a sentence that coordinates unequal ideas by reducing the less important idea to a subordinate phrase.

   | NOT | Mrs. Sinclair is a local author, and she will give a poetry reading next Friday. |
   | BUT | Mrs. Sinclair, a local author, will give a poetry reading next Friday. |

Problem 4: Excessive Coordination

This error will occur if you write long, rambling sentences that contain too many clauses joined by coordinating conjunctions or conjunctive adverbs (*therefore, however, furthermore, moreover, otherwise, then*):

> Twice a week, the girls would ride their bicycles along the paths that followed the river, and they went as far as Brock's Monument; then they turned back, and on their way home they would stop, and they watched the cable car crossing the Whirlpool Rapids.

Revision Strategy

You can correct this error by subordinating some ideas, or, if necessary, by putting them into a separate sentence.

> Twice a week the girls would ride their bicycles along the paths that followed the river, going as far as Brock's Monument before they turned back. On their way home, they would stop and watch the cable car crossing the Whirlpool Rapids.

See Practicing Subordination for more information on how to express less important ideas in subordinate clauses and phrases.

Exercise

Revise the following sentences to correct errors in coordination. Put C beside a correct sentence.

1. All three Bronte sisters, Charlotte, Emily, and Anne, were novelists, and Charlotte Bronte's best-known work is *Jane Eyre*, published in 1847.

   _____

2. Interest rates have increased in the last month, and the Bergmanns are concerned about increased mortgage payments.

   _____

3. I was reading a magazine. I came across an article. It was about pet boa constrictors. It was fascinating.

   _____

4. Beth has good intentions, and sometimes they get her into trouble.

   _____

5. At first Marika agreed to write a letter of recommendation for Michael, and he asked her for the letter, and she refused.

   _____

6. Fred Astaire is best remembered for his dancing expertise, but he also received critical acclaim for his non-dancing role as a scientist in *On the Beach*.

   _____

7. Alonzo is a caring but considerate person.

   _____

8. Isaac was sitting under a tree one day, and an apple fell and hit him on the head, and suddenly he remembered that he had left an apple pie baking in the oven.

   _____

9. Barry wanted to study music at the local community college; however, he couldn't afford to quit work to become a full-time student.

---

10. Charles Darwin was a nineteenth-century English naturalist, and he originated the theory of evolution by natural selection.

Practicing Subordination

Principle

The purpose of **subordination**, as its name suggests, is to show that one idea or fact is less important than another.

Subordination gives you a wider range of sentence structures and conjunctions to choose from than does coordination, where you give equal emphasis to the ideas you join. The wider range available through subordination can give your writing more precision and conciseness. For these reasons, you will probably use more subordination than coordination in most things you write.

COORDINATION	I read the article and I learned about primate behaviour.
SUBORDINATION	When I read the article, I learned about primate behaviour.
SUBORDINATION	I learned about primate behaviour because I read the article.

Basic Rule

Put the more important idea in the main clause. Put the less important idea in a subordinate clause or phrase.

Using Subordinate Conjunctions

You can change a main clause to a subordinate clause by introducing it with a subordinate conjunction such as *because, although, when, while, since, as, provided that, in order that, unless, until.*

Suppose that you wanted to join these two sentences:

Donna scored the winning goal in overtime. She was assured a place on the team.

There is an implied cause and effect relationship between these two sentences—Donna got a place on the team because she scored the winning goal.

Getting a place on the team is more important than scoring the winning goal, so it should go in the main clause.

> Because Donna scored the winning goal in overtime, she was assured a place on the team.

To give the idea in the main clause maximum emphasis, put this clause last in the sentence, as in the example above. On the other hand, if you want to even out the emphasis in the two clauses, put the subordinate clause last.

> Donna was assured a place on the team because she scored the winning goal in overtime.

Punctuation Note 1:
When the subordinate clause comes first in the sentence, put a comma between it and the main clause.

> When psychologists reveal more of their personal reactions, clients are encouraged to be more open.

When the subordinate clause comes second and contains essential information, do not put a comma between it and the main clause.

> Clients are encouraged to be more open when psychologists reveal more of their personal reactions.

Exercise 1

Combine these pairs of sentences by making one sentence a subordinate clause. Be sure to punctuate each sentence correctly. (Hint: Avoid the coordinate conjunctions *and, but, or, nor, for, yet, so.*)

1. Alexander loves to skate.
   He doesn't often get the chance.

   _____

2. He spends most of his time working.
   He has just started his own small business.

   _____

3. He opened a small appliance repair shop.
   He did some market research on consumer demands.

   _____

4. He will be successful.
   He can solve his problems with part-time employees.

   _____

5. He probably won't go skating again.
   He has to get his business under control.

   _____

Changing Main Clauses to Relative Clauses

Relative clauses are introduced with the pronouns *who*, *which*, and *that*. There are two kinds of relative clauses: restrictive and non-restrictive.

Restrictive relative clauses provide information that is necessary to identify the subject of the main clause. Clauses introduced with *that* are usually restrictive.

> Old buildings **that** have not been declared historic sites are in danger of demolition.

Non-restrictive relative clauses provide additional or supplementary information. Clauses introduced with *which* are usually non-restrictive.

> The old downtown library, **which** has not been declared a historic site, is in danger of demolition.

Suppose you wanted to use subordination to join these two sentences:

> Alice Munro is a well-known Canadian writer.
> She has published many short stories in *The New Yorker*.

To join these sentences, you would need to decide which idea you wanted to emphasize: the idea that Alice Munro is a well-known Canadian writer or the idea that she has published many short stories in *The New Yorker*. The resulting sentences could look like this:

> Alice Munro, who is a well-known Canadian writer, has published many short stories in *The New Yorker*.
> Alice Munro, who has published many short stories in *The New Yorker*, is a well-known Canadian writer.

Punctuation Note 2:
Put commas before and after a non-restrictive relative clause. Do not put commas around a restrictive relative clause.

NON-RESTRICTIVE	Alexis, who is recovering from surgery, needs to rest.
RESTRICTIVE	Patients who are recovering from surgery need to rest.

91

Exercise 2

Combine the following pairs of sentences by changing one sentence to a relative clause.

1. My oldest friend lives in Moncton.
   She is coming to spend a month with me this summer.

   _____

2. Some people plan carefully for retirement.
   They experience fewer emotional and financial hardships.

   _____

3. My car is now ten years old.
   It is starting to have serious mechanical problems.

   _____

4. Annalise is now in first year university.
   She is living in a big city for the first time.

   _____

5. Pets are bought as Christmas presents.
   They are often brought to the SPCA before New Year's Day.

   _____

Reducing Subordinate Clauses to Phrases

Sometimes you can make your writing more concise by reducing a subordinate clause to an introductory phrase:

> **Because Donna scored the winning goal in overtime,** she was assured a place on the team.
> **Having scored the winning goal in overtime,** Donna was assured a place on the team.

Punctuation Note 3:
Put a comma after an introductory phrase of more than five words. Put a comma after a shorter introductory phrase if the comma improves the clarity of the sentence.

> **During the night,** workers became increasingly alarmed by peculiar sounds coming from the boiler room.

You can also reduce relative clauses to brief explanatory phrases:

> Alice Munro, who is a well-known Canadian writer, has published many short stories in *The New Yorker*.
> Alice Munro, a well-known Canadian writer, has published many short stories in *The New Yorker*.

Punctuation Note 4:
When the explanatory phrase is non-restrictive because it provides additional information, put commas around it. When the phrase is restrictive because it provides essential information, do not put commas around it.

NON-RESTRICTIVE	Jill Simpson, suffering from hypothermia, needs immediate medical attention.
RESTRICTIVE	People suffering from hypothermia need immediate medical attention.

Exercise 3

Combine the following pairs of sentences by changing one sentence to a subordinate clause. Then reduce this clause to a phrase.

1. Dr. Hackett was our family physician for many years.
   She has recently retired.

   _____

   _____

2. Larry has just got his driver's licence.
   He is willing to drive anywhere at any time.

   _____

   _____

3. Alice left the sales meeting feeling quite optimistic.
   She had made a good presentation.

   _____

   _____

4. Cities are experiencing an economic boom.
   They suffer from a shortage of affordable housing.

   _____

   _____

5. Some employees have poor reading and writing skills.
   They see no future for themselves with a company.

   _____

   _____

Exercise 4: Punctuation Review

Add commas in the appropriate places in the following sentences. Write C beside a correct sentence.

1. Sidney Singh who just got his papers as a journeyman welder was among the three workers injured in the oil rig fire.
2. Even though Susan had looked forward to the holiday for months she found herself reluctant to pack for the trip.
3. Lawyers who are willing to advertise their services are still in the minority.
4. The school ski trip has been cancelled because the roads are icy and dangerous.
5. Students needing more help with writing skills can attend the workshop this Friday.
6. After hunting in every closet and drawer in the house I finally located my birth certificate.
7. This week's TV guide which I remember leaving on the kitchen table has disappeared again.
8. I found the article that you lent me extremely useful.
9. Call me from work if you get the chance.
10. Unless I hear differently I'll assume that we'll stick to our original agreement.

Exercise 5

Combine the following pairs of sentences by changing one sentence to a subordinate clause or a phrase. Be sure to punctuate each sentence correctly.

1. A family is in distress.
   The family may be advised to seek counselling.

   _____

2. Most people will have trouble with some therapists.
   This therapist tries to impose his or her attitudes and morality.

   _____

3. A therapist may remain hidden and vague.
   He or she can expect closed, untrusting behaviour from clients.

4. One approach to family counselling is very popular.
   This is the systems approach.

   _____

5. Some children are abused.
   They learn to see themselves through the eyes of the abuser.

   _____

6. Many native children were educated in residential schools.
   These schools were thought to promote the assimilation of natives into the dominant culture.

   _____

7. Many Christian missionaries had no desire to adapt to native cultures.
   They wanted to change these cultures completely.

   _____

8. The traditional Indian ways of life remained intact for a time.
   Most Indians saw no reason to adopt a completely different value system such as Christianity.

   _____

9. Spiritual beliefs permeated every aspect of native cultures.
   The destruction of these beliefs threatened the whole culture.

   _____

10. Some Indians converted to Christianity.
    They had to reject much of their own culture.

    _____

Correcting Faulty Subordination

Problem 1: Using the Wrong Conjunction

As and *since* are likely to cause the most problems. Both can be used to express both a time sequence and a cause and effect relationship between ideas. You'll confuse your reader if you seem to be signalling a time relationship when you mean to signal cause and effect.

Revision Strategy

Avoid using *as* and *since* in contexts where they might signal both cause and effect and a time sequence.

CORRECT	As I was exercising, I noticed a strange man peering through the windows.
CONFUSING	As I exercise three times a week, I feel more energetic.
CLEAR	Because I exercise three times a week, I feel more energetic.
CORRECT	Since my mother was a child, she has made dolls.
CONFUSING	Since my mother's vision has deteriorated, she no longer sews.
CLEAR	Because my mother's vision has deteriorated, she no longer sews.

Problem 2: Attaching the Right Conjunction to the Wrong Clause

Be sure to attach the subordinate conjunction to the clause containing the dependent or less important idea.

NOT	Karl fell off his bicycle because he broke his arm.
BUT	Because Karl fell off his bicycle, he broke his arm.
NOT	Even though *Francis the Talking Mule* is being telecast instead, the television magazine lists *Casablanca* for 9:00 p.m.
BUT	Even though the television magazine lists *Casablanca* for 9:00 p.m., *Francis the Talking Mule* is being telecast instead.

Problem 3: Excessive Subordination

Using too many subordinate clauses produces a weak, sometimes confusing, sentence.

When we visited Moorea, where we stayed for a week, we drove to a lookout point on Mount Belvedere because we wanted to see the magnificent view of two bays, which are Cook's Bay and Oponohu Bay.

Be careful not to write monster sentences jammed with too many subordinate clauses, like this one:

When we visited Maui, we planned to see the crater of the extinct volcano Haleakala, although we didn't reach the crater on our first try because the road between the visitor centre and the summit was too icy to permit further travel so that naturally we were disappointed although we did make the trip again the next day and were rewarded with beautiful weather and an excellent view of the crater.

Revision Strategies

1. You could revise the first sentence by changing some of the clauses to phrases:

> When we visited Moorea for a week, we drove to the lookout point on Mount Belvedere to see the magnificent view of Cook's Bay and Oponohu Bay.

2. The best way to revise the second sentence is to locate the main points and express them in separate sentences.

> When we visited Maui, we planned to see the crater of the extinct volcano Haleakala. We didn't reach the crater on our first day because the road between the visitor centre and the summit was too icy to permit further travel. Naturally we were disappointed. When we made the trip the next day, however, we were rewarded with beautiful weather and an excellent view of the crater.

Exercise

Revise the following sentences to eliminate errors in subordination. Write C beside a correct sentence.

1. It was pouring rain even though Carlos decided to go for his run.

_____

2. In 1951 Pär Lagerkvist was a Swedish author who won the Nobel Prize for Literature and who wrote the novel *Barabbas*.

_____

3. In 1793, while he was on a boating expedition, the purpose of which was to explore part of the British Columbia coast, able seaman John Carter of H.M.S. *Discovery* died after he suffered the effects of eating mussels that were poisonous.

_____

4. Carter was buried in a bay that is situated about twenty-five kilometres southwest of the cove where the mussels had been found so that Captain George Vancouver later named the two locations Poison Cove and Carter Bay.

_____

5. Since I have known you, I have never seen you looking better.

_____

6. T. S. Eliot once worked as a bank clerk who was a noted poet and literary critic.

_____

7. As Theo was playing the stereo too loudly, he didn't hear his friend knocking at the door.

_____

8. Because today is your birthday, we'll eat at whichever restaurant you choose.

_____

9. The apple tree had an early infestation of tent caterpillars, even though it produced an excellent crop.

_____

10. When you write sentences, write them so that they are clear and concise with no excess verbiage or unnecessary words. [Reduce this construction to a four-word sentence.]

_____

Review Exercise 3: Faulty Coordination and Subordination

Correct any errors in coordination and subordination in the following sentences. Put C beside a correct sentence.

1. Much advertising for computers seems to be designed to appeal to people who want to become business executives, although it does not appeal to people without this aspiration.

_____

2. One ad, which has a setting like a luxurious boardroom, shows several robots which have shiny metal bodies and glowing eyes that are sitting around a conference table.

_____

3. This ad suggests that computers will control the future. It also suggests that computers are powerful, like company executives. This ad might appeal to some people.

_____

4. This ad has different associations for people who do not aspire to corporate power, and they might not find it appealing.

_____

5. The robots suggest that computers are either shiny toys or menacing aliens, not efficient tools.

_____

6. As many people would consider the robots cold and inhuman, they would not be likely to buy a computer.

_____

7. If the company wants to sell more computers, which must be its goal, since that is the company's business, it should promote its products, when it advertises, whether in print or on television, in ways that appeal to everyone.

_____

8. This advertising would have to convince all consumers that computers are no more intimidating than washing machines, lawn mowers, and microwave ovens.

_____

9. Designing such advertising will not be easy; consequently, sales will increase.

_____

10. More consumers will lose their fear of computers, and they will discover another great labour-saving device.

_____

Practicing Parallelism

Principle

The principle of **parallelism** is that similar ideas should be expressed in similar grammatical forms. Parallelism is especially important in a sentence or a paragraph in which you are presenting a series of ideas. All the items in this series should be grammatically parallel.

Basic Rules

1. Keep a list of words grammatically parallel.

PARALLEL ADJECTIVES	Children need emotional support to become **self-confident, secure,** and **healthy** adults.
PARALLEL NOUNS	A person experiencing the immediate aftermath of a marriage breakdown needs **encouragement,** legal **advice,** and practical **assistance.**
PARALLEL ADVERBS	Alice walked **quickly, quietly,** and **apprehensively** towards the parked car.

2. Keep a series of phrases grammatically parallel.

PARALLEL PREPOSITIONAL PHRASES	Anne looked **under the bed, behind the bureau,** and **inside the closet** for her missing pet iguana.
PARALLEL PARTICIPIAL PHRASES	Your duties as a chambermaid include **changing the beds, cleaning the bathrooms,** and **dusting the furniture.**
PARALLEL INFINITIVE PHRASES	On my holidays, I plan **to read mystery novels, catch up on the soap operas,** and **forget about school.**

3. Keep clauses grammatically parallel.

PARALLEL SUBORDINATE CLAUSES	**Where he goes, what he does,** and **whom he sees** are his own business.
PARALLEL MAIN CLAUSES CLAUSES	**I will not be** home tonight, but **my brother will babysit.**

Exercise

Fill in the blanks in the following sentences.

1. He is a victim of corporate mismanagement, government incompetence, and (he was greedy) _HIS OWN GREED_.

100

2. This is probably the most boring, self-indulgent, and (it exploited the audience) _exploitive_ movie I have ever seen.
3. Buying a dog is one thing; (to look after it) _looking after it_ is another.
4. Either get your car fixed or (you should consider selling it and buying a new one) _sell it and buy a new one_
5. The victims of the earthquake were without food, clean water, and (they had nowhere to live) _nowhere to live_.
6. Shelters for battered women and their children provide a safe environment where a woman can sort out her life and (she needs to make important decisions) _make important decisions_.
7. Psychiatrists need to be clear about whether they are serving the best interests of the patient or (the family's needs also have to be considered) _____.
8. I need a job that is interesting, secure, and (lots of money)_____.
9. During the evacuation, children were taken from their parents and (they lived with the strangers they were sent to) _____.
10. By the end of the performance, nearly everyone in the audience had either left or (they were sleeping) _____.

Correcting Faulty Parallelism

Problem

Faulty parallelism occurs whenever words, phrases, or clauses in a series are not grammatically similar. Faulty parallelism often produces sentences that are wordy and awkward. Sometimes they are unclear as well.

> The marathon is a test of strength, being able to endure, and self-discipline.
> After completing her degree, Lydia plans to work as a personnel generalist for several years, move into management, and finally opening her own consulting firm.
> We don't know where the plane will land and no one has told us who is on board.

Revision Strategies

1. Use the same part of speech for a series of words.

PARALLEL NOUNS   A marathon is a test of **strength, endurance,** and **self-discipline.**

2. Use grammatically parallel phrases. Don't mix infinitive and participial phrases in the same sentence.

> PARALLEL INFINITIVE PHRASES
> After completing her degree, Lydia plans **to work** as a personnel generalist for several years, **move** into management, and finally **open** her own consulting firm.

3. Use grammatically parallel clauses. Don't mix subordinate and main clauses in a series.

> PARALLEL CLAUSES
> We don't know **where the plane will land** or **who is on board.**

4. If necessary, repeat an article, a preposition, or a subordinate conjunction.

For coffee break she had **a** cup of tea, **a** muffin, and **an** orange.

"The fault, dear Brutus, lies not **in** our stars, but **in** ourselves, that we are underlings." (William Shakespeare)

People sometimes eat not **because** they are hungry but **because** they are bored.

5. When you are using correlative conjunctions such as *either/or, neither/nor, not only/but also,* be sure that what follows the first conjunction is in the same grammatical form as what follows the second conjunction.

> NOT
> You can either write a thesis or additional courses can be taken to complete this degree program.
>
> BUT
> You can either **write a thesis** or **take additional courses** to complete this degree program.

> NOT
> He is both critical and his arrogance is annoying.
>
> BUT
> He is annoying because he is both **critical** and **arrogant**.

6. When you are using *than* and *as* to form comparisons, be sure the comparison is logical.

> NOT
> Harold's rent payments are actually lower than his car.
>
> BUT
> Harold's rent payments are actually lower than his car payments.

7. Don't try too hard to be parallel. You will sometimes have to present several ideas that cannot be expressed in equivalent grammatical forms. In that situation, separate the ideas into two sentences.

> NOT
> The house is spacious, comfortable, well-appointed, and elegantly draped.
>
> BUT
> The house is spacious, comfortable, and well-appointed. It also has elegant drapes.

Exercise 1

Below are sentences containing faulty parallelism. A revised sentence has been started for you. Complete the revision so that the sentence elements are parallel.

1. Tell Heather that my phone number is in the book and would she please call me tonight.
   Tell Heather that my phone number is in the book and that I
   _____.

2. She not only returned the car with an empty tank, but the back fender had been dented.
   Not only did she _____ but she also
   _____.

3. Stephen will either visit his parents in Ontario this summer or his parents will come to British Columbia.
   Either _____
   or his parents will come to British Columbia.

4. Max is more skilled but has less dependability than Henry.
   Max is more skilled but less _____.

5. When you go out, be sure to lock the door and the key can be left under the mat.
   When you go out, be sure to lock the door and leave _____.

Exercise 2

Revise the following sentences to make elements parallel. Write C beside a correct sentence.

1. The guests at the inn were disturbed by the sound of baying dogs and cats that were howling.

   _____

2. The road was closed because of heavy accumulations of snow and there was ice.

   _____

3. Melissa prefers owning a condominium to when she rented an apartment.

   _____

4. Gertrude says that she would like to see the movie but not having enough money this week.

   _____

5. Pottery bowls are both practical and they are decorative.

_____

6. The stranger refused to tell the townspeople where he had come from, why he was there, or how long he intended to stay.

_____

7. The customer ordered an egg sandwich, glass of milk, and a piece of pumpkin pie.

_____

8. The boys took a short cut by climbing over the fence and crossed the field.

_____

9. If you survive the trials and tribulations of registration day, you will likely survive the year.

_____

10. This is a tale not of heroes and kings but ordinary men.

_____

11. Fernando was hired because he is the best-qualified candidate for the position and he has excellent references from previous employers.

_____

12. This year we are building a deck, laying sod, and we'll plant a few trees.

_____

13. The battery is low, the tires are worn, and a chip in the left headlight.

_____

14. The world would be a better place if the thinkers talked more and the talkers thought more.

_____

15. The day care centre provides stimulating activities and nutritious meals for the children and every worker having a diploma from a community college.

_____

Correcting Mixed Constructions

Mixed constructions are the result of trying to write two different types of sentences at the same time. There are several common kinds of errors that produce mixed constructions.

Problem 1: Using a Subordinate Clause After a Linking Verb

Examples
One example of Del's growing maturity **is when** she starts to see her mother with more detachment.
The main reason for most strikes **is because** the two sides cannot reach a wage settlement.

Revision Strategy

Replace the subordinate clause with a noun or with a clause that functions as a noun.

One example of Del's growing maturity is **her ability** to see her mother with more detachment.
The main reason for most strikes is **the inability** of the two sides to reach a wage settlement.
or
The main reason for most strikes is **that** the two sides cannot reach a wage settlement.

Problem 2: Leaving out the Subject

Example
In *Betrayed*, by playwright Harold Pinter, presents a complex portrayal of friendship between two men.

Revision Strategy

Do not use a prepositional phrase, such as *in the book, in the article, in the film*, as the subject of a sentence. You could revise the sentence above by either removing the preposition *in* (so that *Betrayed* becomes the subject of the sentence) or by adding a subject.

Betrayed, by playwright Harold Pinter, presents a complex portrayal of friendship between two men.
or
In *Betrayed*, playwright Harold Pinter presents a complex portrayal of friendship between two men.

Problem 3: Not Following Through a Pattern with Coordinate Conjunctions

Examples
Wanting a third piece of pizza, but she was trying to stay on her diet.
Unwilling to face reality, for he was afraid of failure.

Revision Strategy

If you are using one of the coordinate conjunctions (*and, but, or, nor, for, yet, so*) to join main clauses, be sure that both clauses are complete.

She wanted a third piece of pizza, but she was trying to stay on her diet.
He was unwilling to face reality, for he was afraid of failure.

Problem 4: Not Following Through a Pattern with Paired Conjunctions

Examples
I have neither the inclination and I don't have the time to talk to you right now.
Bill must either pay his parking tickets or he might be arrested.

Revision Strategy

If you are using the paired conjunctions *either/or, neither/nor, not only/but also, both/and* to join words, clauses, or phrases, be sure what follows the second conjunction is grammatically parallel to what follows the first.

I have neither **the inclination** nor **the time** to talk to you right now.
Bill must either **pay his parking tickets** or **risk being arrested.**

Problem 5: Failing to Follow Through a Pattern with a Comparison

Examples
The more I try to communicate with her, I don't seem to be able to make much contact.
The less work I do for this course, I feel worse about catching up.

Revision Strategy

If you begin a sentence with a phrase such as *the more, the less, the better, the further*, complete the comparison. You might pair *the more* with *the better* or with *the less*; you might pair *the less* with *the worse*.

The more I try to communicate with her, **the less** contact I seem to make.
The less work I do for this course, **the worse** I feel about catching up.

Problem 6: Putting in Too Many Conjunctions

Examples
Although Sally was an inexperienced skier, **yet** she was never afraid to tackle the most demanding slopes.
Because Marco never hesitates to ask a question, **therefore** he learns more in class.

Revision Strategy

Avoid using two conjunctions that mean the same thing to join two clauses. *Although, yet, however,* and *but* all have the same meaning, as do *because, therefore,* and *for*. Eliminate one of the conjunctions.

Although Sally was an inexperienced skier, she was never afraid to tackle the most demanding slopes.
or
Sally was an inexperienced skier, yet she was never afraid to tackle the most demanding slopes.

Because Marco never hesitates to ask a question, he learns more in class.
or
Marco never hesitates to ask a question; therefore he learns more in class.

Problem 7: Mixing a Question and a Statement

Example

He wondered will my old car last another year?

Revision Strategies

1. Convert the question to direct speech.

   He wondered, "Will my old car last another year?"

2. Make both parts of the sentence statements.

   He wondered whether his old car would last another year.

Exercise

Revise the following sentences to correct mixed constructions. This time there aren't any correct sentences.

1. Although he knew that smoking was harmful, however, he continued to smoke two packs a day.

   _____

2. Without confirmed hotel reservations and a return ticket means a traveller won't get past immigration officials at the island's international airport.

   _____

3. The driveway hasn't been poured yet is the reason we have to park on the street.

   _____

4. To put something over on people is when you trick or deceive them.

   _____

5. This movie appeals to both critics as well as the general public.

   _____

6. I don't know how much will it cost to repair the furnace.

   _____

7. One reason why this child has trouble learning is because she doesn't get enough to eat.

   _____

8. It wasn't until Paula reached the front door of the Smiths' house before she realized that the party was the following Saturday.

9. I'll let you decide whether to order pizza or do you prefer Chinese food?

10. Lynne was more interested in reading a novel rather than in watching reruns of *Gilligan's Island*.

11. To put up with something you don't like it means you tolerate it.

12. In the photograph taken by the undercover police officer shows the accused accepting a package from a known mobster.

13. The more books I read, I don't seem to remember much.

14. Fortunately, he's the type of student who both knows his work and he cares about it.

15. Because he's tired today is why Jimmy is cranky.

16. The enclosed directions are how to put the model together.

17. Learning to skate as a child is easier than when you learn to skate as an adult.

18. Because their son's baseball tournament is this weekend, the Malaks therefore won't be going to the lake.

19. I should either revise this essay completely or starting over again with a different topic is a possibility.

_____

20. Dermabelle Products is sending out questionnaires asking consumers as to how they rate the company's soap.

_____

Review Exercise 4: Faulty Parallelism and Mixed Constructions

Correct any sentences containing faulty parallelism or mixed constructions. Put C beside a correct sentence.

1. Every year thousands of Canadians miss work and school is also missed because of the flu.

_____

2. Flu symptoms vary, but they often include a high fever, the throat is sore, a sense of lightheadedness, and many people have aching bodies and nausea.

_____

3. The reason for the illness is because of a virus that attacks the respiratory system.

_____

4. Although many people get the flu, however, few people die from it.

_____

5. Today's situation is markedly different from that following World War I, when an epidemic of Spanish Flu struck Canada as well as other parts of the world.

_____

6. Not only were there many more cases of flu, a much higher proportion caused death.

_____

7. An example is when the rate was one death in one thousand cases in the flu epidemics of the early nineteeth century.

_____

8. In contrast, the mortality rate in the flu epidemic of 1919-1923 was close to one in forty: Québec had 530 704 cases and 13 880 deaths by the end of 1919; and 8705 out of an estimated 300 000 cases in Ontario.

_____

9. You may wonder what would we do if such a deadly epidemic struck again?

_____

10. The more we try to carry on with our daily lives when we have the flu, we are more likely to spread the disease.

_____

Review Exercise 5: General Review of Sentence Structure

Revise the following sentences to eliminate fragments, comma faults, fused sentences, dangling and misplaced modifiers, non-parallel elements, faulty subordination and coordination, and mixed constructions. Write C beside a correct sentence.

1. Holding the leash firmly, the dog was led across the street.

_____

2. Watch your step the sidewalk is very slippery.

_____

3. Sam, the last person anyone thought would drop out of school.

_____

4. The finish on the car is both beautiful and it is durable.

_____

5. The dishwasher doesn't work, you'll have to call a repair shop.

_____

111

6. Swimming strongly to shore, the drowning child was saved by the lifeguard.

_____

7. A good example of Marika's thoughtfulness is when she shops for an elderly neighbour.

_____

8. Ned hesitated for a moment then he jumped into the icy water and swam to the raft.

_____

9. Robert only has ten dollars to last until payday.

_____

10. After the plane had landed and we had picked up the luggage, standing in a seemingly endless line, waiting to clear customs.

_____

11. Angie maintains that the key to a healthy life is a balanced diet, regular exercise, and she meditates daily.

_____

12. Residents are asked to restrict their use of water during the dry spell, otherwise, the city will impose water rationing.

_____

13. We are sold out of that particular video game, and we expect a new shipment early next week.

_____

14. Kent was trying to bring contraband goods into Canada because he was stopped at the border.

_____

15. Although Jed rarely cooks, he is an expert at making one dish: barbecued steak.

_____

16. Circling high over the copse of trees, Jeanette watched the hawk.

_____

17. Seldom allowing his personal problems to interfere with his work, so he was respected by everyone.

_____

18. It was the first day of the summer break Trudy knew exactly how she would spend the afternoon.

_____

19. Shouting frantically, the car rolled down the hill with Boris in hot pursuit.

_____

20. Boris was furious with himself, he had forgotten to set the hand brake when he parked.

_____

21. Fortunately, the car sustained only minor damage when it landed in a grass-filled ditch.

_____

22. After careful consideration, the little boy announced that he wanted only one thing for his birthday. A Teenage Mutant Ninja Turtle.

_____

23. After completing her diploma, Christine plans to work for a few years, saving her money, and finally she wants to open her own consulting firm.

_____

24. Her hand numb from writing, Janet finished the exam just as the bell sounded.

_____

25. As he swung the watch slowly back and forth, the volunteer from the audience stood transfixed before the magician.

_____

26. Loretta has a bad case of influenza, and she has been off work for a week.

_____

27. The referee did not call a penalty even though the player was clearly guilty of highsticking.

_____

28. The names have been changed to protect the innocent, however, all events described in the story are true.

_____

29. Vanessa not being a person I would trust to keep a secret.

_____

30. Since the insurance has expired, you won't be able to drive the car.

_____

Recognizing Auxiliary Verbs

In some constructions, the verb is only one word.

I **am** here.
We **went** to a movie.

In other constructions, the verb consists of a group of words called a **verb phrase.**

I **have been** here since five o'clock.
We **will go** to a movie tonight.

A verb phrase is formed by joining one or more **auxiliary** verbs and a **main verb**: *will be running, has been stolen.* The last word in the **verb phrase** is the main verb; the other words in the phrase are auxiliaries.

I **have been waiting** here for some time. [*Waiting* is the main verb; *have* and *been* are auxiliaries.]
We **should have gone** to a movie last night. [*Gone* is the main verb; *should* and *have* are auxiliaries.]

The following words can be used as auxiliary verbs:

1. forms of **to be**: *am, is, are, was, were, be, been, being*
2. forms of **to have**: *have, has, had*
3. forms of **to do**: *do, does, did*
4. other auxiliaries: *can, could, may, might, must, shall, will, should, would, ought to, have to, supposed to, used to*

Exercise: Recognizing Auxiliary Verbs

In each sentence, underline the complete verb phrase and circle the auxiliary verbs. **Note:** *Not* is an adverb. It is not part of the verb phrase.

1. Petra has written her last exam.
2. We should have heard from Alice by now.
3. Grandfather is used to eating his supper in front of the TV.
4. The Singhs will be going to the Bahamas for Christmas.
5. Ralph did not submit his application until after the deadline.
6. Sonya has been visiting a sick friend all afternoon.
7. I would be going home for Christmas if I had enough money.
8. Ramon might have gotten a promotion by now.
9. I have to cook dinner for twelve people tonight.
10. The car radio must have been stolen last night.

Common Problems with Auxiliaries

Using the Present Participle as the Main Verb

The **present participle** of both regular and irregular verbs is formed by adding *ing* to the present tense: *running, walking, breathing, dancing*. When the present participle is used without an auxiliary, it does not function as a verb. Instead, it functions as a noun or an adjective.

> *Dancing* is good exercise. [*Dancing* is a noun.]
> The *dancing* bear is the star of the circus. [*Dancing* is an adjective describing *bear*.]
> The groom is *dancing* with his mother-in-law. [*Is dancing* is the verb.]

Exercise 1

Write *N* beside a sentence in which the present participle is used as a noun, *Adj* beside a sentence in which it is used as an adjective, and *V* beside a sentence in which it is used as a verb. Underline the complete verb in each sentence.

1. Downhill skiing used to be his favourite sport.
2. We ought to hold our annual skating party on New Year's Day.
3. Charles is being especially helpful today.
4. Painting and sculpting classes will be held at the art gallery this winter.
5. I will be cleaning out the basement all afternoon.

If you use the present participle (*dancing, singing, running*) as though it were a complete verb, you'll write a sentence fragment.

NOT   Marvin **drinking** the last beer in the house.

BUT   Marvin **drank** the last beer in the house.

Be especially careful to avoid using *being* as a verb.

NOT   The donated clothes **being** wet and dirty.

BUT   The donated clothes **are** [were] wet and dirty.

Avoid constructions in which *being that* is used to mean *because*.

NOT   I was late **being that** I had a flat tire.

BUT   I was late **because** I had a flat tire.

Exercise 2

In each sentence below, change the present participle to a complete verb. You can add an auxiliary verb to the present participle (*is running*) or you can use another tense of the verb (*ran*).

1. Carol's new car being a red MG with a silver racing stripe.

2. To prepare for the track meet next month, Chris running five kilometres every day.

3. All of Lynne's friends waiting in the darkened room to yell "Surprise!" when she opens the door.

4. All the exercise shoes in the store costing at least fifty dollars.

5. That amount being the price you have to pay for good runners these days.

Confusing the Past Tense and the Past Participle

1. Do **not** use an auxiliary with the simple past tense.

> NOT   The instructor **has came** into class five minutes late every day this week.

> BUT   The instructor **has come** into class five minutes late every day this week.
> **or**
> The instructor **came** into class five minutes late every day this week.

2. **Do** use an auxiliary with a past participle.

> NOT   We **seen** him take the money.

> BUT   We **have seen** him take the money.
> **or**
> We **saw** him take the money.

> NOT   He **run** the business alone for five years.

> BUT   He **has run** the business alone for five years.
> **or**
> He **ran** the business alone for five years.

Exercise 3

Correct the errors in the use of verbs in the following sentences.

1. Sidney has went to visit his fiancee in Waterloo.

_____

2. Allison has became a highly trained cardiologist.

_____

3. The baby hasn't drank any of his milk yet.

_____

4. When Norm saw smoke coming from the attic, he immediately rung the fire alarm.

_____

5. Mrs. Kishimoto has drove the same route to work every day for years.

_____

118

6. By Boxing Day, the young child had broke half her presents.

_____

7. Marcia was upset because her skirt had shrank.

_____

8. Have you chose a topic for your research paper yet?

_____

9. We seen Wayne Gretzky at a local shopping mall last week.

_____

10. I have tore a hole in my new sweater.

_____

Using *Of* to Mean *Have*

Of is a preposition, not a verb or an auxiliary.

NOT	I *could of done* better.
BUT	I *could have done* better.

Using Too Many *Woulds*

This error usually occurs in conditional statements of the *if . . . then* sort. Don't put *would* in the clause beginning with *if*.

NOT	If I **would have known** the way, I wouldn't have needed to ask for directions.
BUT	If I **had known** the way, I wouldn't have needed to ask for directions.

Exercise 4

Correct all errors in the use of auxiliaries in the following sentences. Put C beside a correct sentence.

1. I might of guessed it was you.

_____

2. If I would have phoned the airport, I would have known that the plane was late.

_____

3. Peter would of written if he would have had your address.

_____

4. Paulette ought to of finished her shift by now.

_____

5. Alexis might have tried to reach us.

_____

Exercise 5

Revise the following sentences so that auxiliaries and verb forms are used correctly. Write C beside a correct sentence.

1. If we would have arrived ten minutes earlier, we would have caught the ferry to the mainland.

_____

2. The Browns and the Greenes haven't spoke to each other since the neighbourhood barbecue.

_____

3. The lime-green socks being the only clean pair in the house.

_____

4. You shouldn't of sat beside the "Wet Paint" sign.

_____

5. He come to the conclusion that he will have to do the work himself.

_____

6. After the game the fans rushing on the field to congratulate the players.

_____

7. The award couldn't of gone to a more deserving person.

_____

8. Many of the spectators exclaimed that they had never seen such an electrifying performance.

_____

9. I would have asked you to come to the movie with us if I would have known you weren't busy.

_____

10. Darcy is hanging up his track shoes; he has ran his last race.

_____

Correcting Errors with Irregular Verbs

Problems with irregular verbs fall mainly into two categories:

1. Problems with **form** (knowing, for example, that the principal parts of *to drink* are *drink, drinking, drank, drunk*)
2. Problems with **usage** (knowing, for example, that a person is *hanged* but a picture is *hung*)

We'll look at the forms of irregular verbs and then at the usage of some particularly troublesome irregular verbs.

Verb Forms: Principal Parts

Verbs have four principal parts: the **present tense**, the **past tense**, the **present participle**, and the **past participle**. When you want to name a verb, you give its **infinitive form**, which consists of *to* + the verb: *to run, to breathe, to think.*

To form the past tense and past participle of **regular** verbs, add *ed* to the present tense. To form the present participle, add *ing* to the present tense.

Present	Past	Past Participle	Present Participle
talk	talked	talked	talking
hope	hoped	hoped	hoping
listen	listened	listened	listening

The principal parts of regular verbs are easy to form. **Irregular** verbs are more troublesome. While they do add *ing* to form the present participle, irregular verbs follow different (and unpredictable) patterns to form the past tense and past participle. The following examples show three of these different patterns:

Present	Past	Past Participle
hurt	hurt	hurt [All forms are the same.]
dig	dug	dug [The past tense and past participle are formed by an internal vowel change.]
rise	rose	risen [All three forms are different.]

If you are uncertain about the principal parts of any verb, check a good dictionary. For a regular verb, usually only the present tense is given. You know how to form the principal parts of this verb by using the regular pattern. For some irregular verbs, such as *pay*, a second form will be given in parentheses (*paid*). This form serves as both the past tense and the past participle. For irregular verbs that have three different forms, such as *go*, both the past tense (*went*) and the past participle (*gone*) will appear in parentheses.

Exercise 1: Principal Parts of Irregular Verbs

Complete the following chart of irregular verb forms. Use a dictionary for reference. You will notice that some verbs have alternate forms for the past tense and/or past participle. The past tense of *dive*, for example, is *dived* or *dove*.

Infinitive	Past Tense	Past Participle
EXAMPLE: to run	ran	run
1. to be	_____	_____
2. to beat	_____	_____
3. to bear	_____	_____
4. to become	_____	_____
5. to begin	_____	_____
6. to bind	_____	_____
7. to buy	_____	_____
8. to burst	_____	_____
9. to catch	_____	_____
10. to choose	_____	_____
11. to cling	_____	_____

12. to come _____ _____
13. to cost _____ _____
14. to dive _____ _____
15. to do _____ _____
16. to dream _____ _____
17. to drink _____ _____
18. to eat _____ _____
19. to fall _____ _____
20. to fly _____ _____
21. to forgive _____ _____
22. to freeze _____ _____
23. to get _____ _____
24. to go _____ _____
25. to grind _____ _____
26. to hit _____ _____
27. to hold _____ _____
28. to keep _____ _____
29. to kneel _____ _____
30. to lay _____ _____
31. to lead _____ _____
32. to leave _____ _____
33. to lie _____ _____
34. to lose _____ _____
35. to prove _____ _____
36. to read _____ _____
37. to ride _____ _____
38. to rise _____ _____
39. to see _____ _____
40. to set _____ _____
41. to shake _____ _____
42. to shoot _____ _____
43. to show _____ _____
44. to sing _____ _____
45. to speak _____ _____
46. to stand _____ _____
47. to swim _____ _____
48. to take _____ _____
49. to teach _____ _____
50. to think _____ _____

Exercise 2: Using Irregular Verb Forms Correctly

In each sentence use the correct form of the irregular verb in parentheses.

1. For years we have (fight) _____ for traffic controls to be installed at this intersection.
2. Everyone was relieved when the house guest finally (leave) _____. She had definitely (wear) _____ out her welcome.
3. I think that you have (bite) _____ off more than you can chew.
4. George has (sing) _____ with the band for over five years.
5. Has your uncle (come) _____ back from India yet?
6. We definitely (see) _____ that car run a red light.
7. You won't be able to reach Linda at the office because she will have (leave) _____ by now.
8. If I had (know) _____ what to do, I could have been finished by now.
9. My brothers have (sleep) _____ in a tent in the back yard every night this week.
10. Beth had (swim) _____ across the lake for the first time last summer.
11. I should have (run) _____ for office in the last election.
12. Someone has (drink) _____ all the beer in the fridge.
13. By the time we arrived at the corner, the bus had already (go) _____ .
14. Where have you (hide) _____ the scissors this time?
15. The main problem here (be) _____ that people have lost hope.

Troublesome Verbs

1. *Lie* and *Lay*

To lie, meaning "to recline," and *to lay*, meaning "to place," are perhaps the most commonly confused verbs in English. Here are the principal parts of these verbs:

Present	Past	Past Participle	Present Participle
lie	lay	lain	lying
lay	laid	laid	laying

As you can see, one reason for the confusion is that the present tense of *to lay* is the same as the past tense of *to lie*. The other forms of these verbs are close enough in spelling to add to the confusion.

The following examples illustrate common errors:

George is laying on the couch. [should be *is lying*]

George laid on the couch all afternoon. [should be *lay*]
George has laid on the couch all day. [should be has *lain*]

2. *Lead* and *Led*

Led is the past tense of to *lead*.

NOT   The path they took **lead** to the abandoned cannery.
BUT   The path they took **led** to the abandoned cannery.

3. *Hanged* and *Hung*

When you're referring to hanging an object, the principal parts of *to hang* are *hang, hung, hung, hanging*.

When you're referring to hanging a person, the principle parts of *to hang* are *hang, hanged, hanged, hanging*.

NOT   The condemned man was **hung** at dawn.
BUT   The condemned man was **hanged** at dawn.

4. *Loose* and *Lose*

Loose is usually an adjective, as in loose change, loose clothes, loose talk. *To loose* (meaning "to set free") is a verb, as in "He loosed the dog on the intruders." *To lose* is always a verb. Sometimes *lose* and *loose* are confused, as in these examples:

I am always loosing something. [should be *losing*]
Be careful not to loose your way. [should be *lose your way*]

5. *Choose* and *Chose*

Chose is the past tense of *to choose*.

Today I **choose** to stay at home.
Yesterday I **chose** to stay at home.

6. *Get/Got/Gotten*

Both *got* and *gotten* can be used as the past participle of *to get*.

She has got sick three times this winter.
She has gotten sick three times this winter.

Has got can be used to express both possession and obligation.

OBLIGATION   We have got to leave now.
POSSESSION   Bill has got a new car.

In more formal writing, it is usually better, however, to use *must* to express obligation and *has* or *have* to express possession.

We **must** leave now.
Bill **has** a new car.

7. *Used* and *Supposed*
Remember to use the *ed* ending with both of these verbs.

NOT	I am **suppose** to meet him at six o'clock.
BUT	I am **supposed** to meet him at six o'clock.
NOT	Clara is **use** to getting her own way.
BUT	Clara is **used** to getting her own way.

Exercise 3: Troublesome Verbs
Correct any errors in verb usage in the following sentences. Put C beside a correct sentence.

1. He has lead the Canadian ski team for the past three years.

   _____

2. Paul is use to having problems with math.

   _____

3. Several of the pictures in the exhibition were hanged upside down.

   _____

4. When I bought the computer, I choose the laser over the daisy wheel printer.

   _____

5. Susan will get sunstroke if she lays in the sun much longer.

   _____

6. You are supposed to get that assignment finished by next Wednesday.

   _____

7. By the time Marcus had laid down, it was almost time to get up.

   _____

8. All applications have got to reach this office by June 30.

   _____

9. When you loose work done on a computer, you've lost it forever.

   _____

10. I have laid the book on the table, just as you asked.

_____

Exercise 4: Verb Forms and Troublesome Verbs

Revise the following sentences so that verb forms are used correctly. Write C beside a correct sentence.

1. The car was suppose to be ready today, but the mechanic says that it needs more work.

   supposed , said _____

2. Have you swam in the wave pool at the new recreation centre?

   swum _____

3. I think you have lain out in the sun too long.

   C   laid _____

4. Alan was so thirsty after exercising that he drunk five glasses of water.

   _____ _drank_ _____

5. Marlene looses a contact lense at least once a month.

   ____ _loses_ _____

6. The owner watched as the trainer lead the horse around the paddock.

   _C_ _____

7. If you have a headache, take two aspirins and lay down for half an hour.

   _____ _lie_ _____

8. The room was broken into, but nothing was stolen.

   _C_ _____

9. Witnesses seen someone running from the building just before the fire started.

   saw _____

10. We use to order out for pizza every Friday night.

    used _____

Review Exercise 6: Auxiliaries, Irregular Verbs, and Troublesome Verbs

Correct any errors in verb forms and usage in the following sentences. Some sentences have more than one error. Put C beside a correct sentence.

1. This heap of junk before you use to be a Yamaha 250 Special.

_____

2. If you would of seen it new, you would never have believed it could look the way it looks now.

_____

3. It is rusted from laying beside the garage all winter.

_____

4. Its tires are bald, its seat is ripped, and its left signal light is broke.

_____

5. Its owner use to get angry when it wouldn't start and pound it with a hammer.

_____

6. We seen him chip the paint and dent the gas tank that way.

_____

7. But you should of saw it in its days of glory.

_____

8. It always lead all the other machines on the road, and it would loose them on the corners.

_____

9. People aren't suppose to get sentimental about machines, but I sure do hate to see it lay here, getting more and more run down every year.

_____

10. But I guess that happens to people too.

_____

Using Prepositions with Verbs

Most of the time, especially if English is your first language, you'll know which prepositions go with which verbs. Occasionally, however, you may not be sure. Sometimes there doesn't seem to be any logical reason for using one preposition rather than another; it's just the way prepositions are used in English. For example, we say *agree with the teacher* but *agree to meet*.

To see how good you are at choosing the correct preposition, do the exercise below. If you need more information, see Set Phrases (23a) in *Forms of Writing*. Most dictionaries will also give you this information.

Exercise 1

Add the appropriate preposition to each sentence.

1. This new technique differs _____ older methods in several important ways.
2. The student sat staring into space, bored _____ the lecture.
3. All parties have agreed _____ the amendments made to the contract.
4. Spicy food does not agree _____ her.
5. These chocolate cookies from the bakery compare favourably _____ my home-made cookies.

Exercise 2

Add the appropriate prepositions to each sentence.

1. The two managers differ _____ each other in their analysis of the problem.
2. The children were warned _____ playing baseball too close to the house.
3. Anita participates _____ several extracurricular activities.
4. The expedition finally succeeded _____ reaching the summit of the mountain.
5. When we leave depends _____ how soon you are ready.
6. The patient had to abstain _____ eating for twelve hours before undergoing the medical procedure.
7. He compared my singing voice _____ that of a crow.
8. We know we can count _____ you to get the job done.
9. Let us dispense _____ these matters quickly so that we can move on to the major subject of discussion.
10. The baby has been immunized _____ polio, diphtheria, and whooping cough.

The Passive Voice

Recognizing the Passive Voice

Verbs have two voices: **active** and **passive**.

ACTIVE   Joan and Lloyd **built** the fence.
PASSIVE   The fence **was built** by Joan and Lloyd.

In an active construction, the subject acts; in a passive construction, the subject is acted upon. Active constructions are usually more forceful and concise. Passive constructions tend to be indirect and wordy. For these reasons, the active voice is usually preferable to the passive voice.

Passive constructions are useful, however, whenever you don't know who performed the action or when the receiver of the action is more important than the doer.

The bike **was stolen** last night. [We don't know who stole it.]
Three thousand concert tickets **have been sold**. [Who sold the tickets is unimportant.]

Passive constructions are commonly used in scientific writing and in the minutes of a meeting.

Five litres of solvent **were added** to the mixture.
The motion **was passed** unanimously.

Don't use the passive voice merely to sound more formal.

NOT   An agreement was made by Jack and Kevin to share the costs of repairing the car.
BUT   Jack and Kevin agreed to share the costs of repairing the car.

Also be careful not to mix active and passive constructions in the same sentence when the result is awkward.

NOT   Allie finished the assignment and it was handed in the next morning.
BUT   Allie finished the assignment and handed it in the next morning.

Exercise 1: Recognizing the Passive Voice

Label each sentence *A* (active) or *P* (passive).

1. Dr. Kiley was paged on the hospital intercom.

2. Marika has decided against our proposal.
3. The sun was shining on the sea.
4. A person is usually asked to present at least two pieces of identification when writing a cheque.
5. I was never consulted in this matter.
6. Where have all the flowers gone?
7. All of the flowers have been picked.
8. Many are called but few are chosen.
9. When will I be loved?
10. I have met with the grievance committee three times this month.

Forming the Passive Voice

To form the passive voice, use the appropriate form of the verb **to be** (*is, are, was, were, will be, will have been*) with the **past** participle.

> The trophies **are displayed** in the case. [present tense]
> Timothy **was honoured** at the awards dinner. [past tense]
> The awards **will be presented** tomorrow. [future tense]

Exercise 2: Forming the Passive Voice

Change the following active constructions to passive constructions.

1. Children playing with matches started the fire.

_____

2. Three people who saw smoke and flames coming from a ground floor window sounded the alarm.

_____

3. A police officer who happened upon the scene rescued the children.

_____

4. A dog bit Maxine.

_____

5. Over five hundred people have signed the petition.

_____

Correcting Errors in Subject-Verb Agreement

Problem

An error in subject-verb agreement occurs when a singular subject is matched with a plural verb or when a plural subject is matched with a singular verb, as in these examples:

> **Neither** of the students **feel** enthusiastic about grammar.
> [singular]   [plural]
> **Tapes and clothes is** all she wants.
> [plural]   [singular]
> **Every** doctor and nurse **are** expected to abide by the no-
> [singular]   [plural]
> smoking policy.

Basic Rule

One of the most basic rules in grammar is that **subjects and verbs must agree**. A singular subject takes a singular verb, and a plural subject takes a plural verb.

> Our neighbour's **house is** for sale. [The singular subject *house* agrees with the singular verb *is*.]
> The **children want** their dinner. [The plural subject *children* agrees with the plural verb *want*.]

Most of the time, making subjects and verbs agree is no problem, but there are some tricky situations to watch for. The following guidelines cover most of them.

Singular Subjects

The following types of subjects are **singular** and require **singular verbs**:

1. Titles of publications and works of art:

> *Sons and Lovers* is one of D. H. Lawrence's best-known novels.

2. Some words that are plural in form but singular in meaning, such as *news, physics, politics, measles*:

> **Physics** is a rapidly changing field of study.

3. Collective nouns, such as *band, team, jury, committee,* and *family,* that refer to people or things acting as a single unit:

> Raphael's **family has** decided to move to St. John's.

See also the discussion of collective nouns in Correcting Errors In Pronoun Agreement.

4. Words joined by *and* that refer to a single unit or to the same person:

> **Toast and jam is** his favourite breakfast.
> **My friend and mentor is** a wise and caring person.

5. The following indefinite pronouns are singular and take singular verbs:

everybody	anybody	somebody	nobody	either
everyone	anyone	someone	no one, one	neither
everything	anything	something	nothing	each

> **Everyone has** agreed to a reduction in pay.
> **Nothing is** being done about this problem.

Indefinite pronouns are especially troublesome when they are followed by prepositional phrases such as *of the children, of the workers, of the plans.* Remember that the subject of the sentence is never located in a prepositional phrase.

> **One** of the drivers **was** speeding.
> **Neither** of these proposals **addresses** our needs.

See also the discussion of indefinite pronouns in Correcting Errors In Pronoun Agreement.

6. Singular subjects joined by *or, nor, either/or, neither/nor, not only/but also:*

> **Neither** Ken **nor** Adrienne **has** returned my call.
> **Not only** my paper **but also** my pen **has** disappeared.

When a singular and plural subject are joined by these conjunctions, the subject closer to the verb is the one that counts. It makes the verb either singular or plural. If you are joining a singular and plural subject with these conjunctions, put the plural subject last and make the verb plural.

> **Neither the manager nor the employees agree** with the decision made by the arbitration board.

7. Phrases that express amounts considered as units:

> **Five dollars is** too much to pay to get into a movie on weekdays.
> **Fifteen litres is** enough to fill the gas tank.

8. The expression *the number*:

Do you think **the number** of people who can afford to go to movies **is** decreasing?

9. Subjects preceded by *each* or *every*:

Every resident and business owner **is** expected to participate in the town's annual spring clean-up.

Exercise 1

Correct all errors in subject-verb agreement in the following sentences. Put C beside a correct sentence.

1. Neither of those sandwiches look very appetizing.

_____

2. One of the jewels have been taken from the case.

_____

3. Neither the management nor the employees know how long the strike will last.

_____

4. *The Wars*, a novel by Timothy Findley, were made into a film.

_____

5. The number of unemployed people in this province grow every month.

_____

6. The volunteer group are collecting canned goods for the food bank.

_____

7. Ninety thousand dollars are too much for that vacant lot.

_____

8. Measles are spreading rapidly through this isolated settlement.

_____

9. Bread and butter are delicious by itself or accompanied by mayonnaise, roast beef, lettuce, pickles, and tomatoes.

10. A flock of geese is flying over the pond.

Plural Subjects

The following types of subjects are **plural** and require **plural verbs**:

1. Most subjects joined by *and*:

   Fame and fortune are his chief desires.

2. Collective nouns that refer to people or things acting individually:

   The **audience have differing opinions** on the quality of the performance.

3. Some words that are always plural, such as *trousers* and *scissors*:

   My **scissors** never **seem** to be where I left them.

4. The expression *a number*:

   A number of winners **were** absent from the awards dinner.

5. Irregular plural forms such as *criteria, data,* and *media*:

   The **criteria** for performance appraisals **are** discussed in the manual.

Who, Which, and *That* Agreement Problems

Depending upon the noun or pronoun to which they refer, *who, which,* and *that* may be either singular or plural and therefore take either a singular or plural verb.

   This is the **one movie** this season **that is** certain to appeal to people of all ages.

In this sentence *that* is singular because *movie* is singular. *Is* agrees with *that*.

   These are **movies that appeal** to almost everybody.

Here *that* is plural because *movies* is plural. *Appeal* agrees with *that*.

Special Cases

1. Don't be distracted by words, phrases, or clauses that come between the subject and the verb. These constructions do not affect the agreement between the subject and verb.

   The **actor**, accompanied by his manager and his publicity agent, **is** giving interviews this afternoon.

The team **manager,** along with the coach and the players, **is** protesting the misconduct penalty.

2. In most sentences, the subject comes before the verb, but in some constructions the subject comes **after** the verb. The most common of these constructions are:

- Sentences beginning with *here* and *there.*
  The key thing to remember is that *here* and *there* are **never** the subject of the sentence.

  Here **is my recipe** for mystery meat casserole.
  There **are secret ingredients** which I will never reveal.

- Sentences beginning with long prepositional or participial phrases.

  Deep within the farthest recesses of the cave lives a horrifying monster.
  Plunging through waves five metres high comes an enormous whale.

3. A sentence may contain a plural noun following a linking verb (usually a form of the verb *to be*). This plural noun does **not** govern the verb. If the subject is singular, the verb must be singular.

  The latest **fashion** this year **is** tan shoes and pink shoe laces.

Exercise 2

Underline the correct verb in each sentence.

1. Exercise and nutritious food (is/are) part of a sound fitness program.
2. The finance minister, in consultation with her advisors, (has/have) formulated a new policy.
3. Here (is/are) the books you wanted on management theory and organizational behaviour.
4. Which one of these colas (tastes/taste) better?
5. These are the authors who (is/are) on the list of required readings.
6. *Landscape with Peacocks*, which Paul Gauguin painted in 1892, (is/are) housed in the Pushkin Museum in Moscow.
7. His favourite snack (is/are) pretzels and champagne.
8. Around the curve in the road (is/are) a large boulder placed by King Kamehameha I.
9. Every application and résumé (has been/have been) reviewed.
10. A number of athletes (has/have) withdrawn from the competition.

Exercise 3: Subject-Verb Agreement

Correct all errors in subject-verb agreement in the sentences below. Put *C* beside a correct sentence.

1. Mohandas Gandhi (1869-1948) is one of the many religious and political leaders who has been assassinated during this century.

_____

2. Gandhi, like his American follower Martin Luther King, were convinced that changes in political systems could be brought about by nonviolent protest.

_____

3. In South Africa, where Gandhi spent several years, his fight for Indian rights were partially successful.

_____

4. In India, the number of people unhappy with British rule were increasing.

_____

5. There was two methods of resistance Gandhi advocated: nonviolent noncooperation and mass civil disobedience.

_____

6. Neither of these methods were workable without the basic decency of the British, who were reluctant to fire on unarmed civilians.

_____

7. An army of unarmed women, men, and children was not an appropriate enemy.

_____

8. Gandhi's attempts to unite Hindus and Muslims after India gained independence was not popular with everyone.

_____

9. Somebody who disagreed with his policies were unhappy enough to kill him.

_____

10. Neither Gandhi nor Martin Luther King have been forgotten.

_____

Review Exercise 7: Correcting Errors in Subject-Verb Agreement

Correct all errors in subject-verb agreement. Put C beside a correct sentence.

1. This antique table, in addition to many other pieces of fine furniture, are to be sold at an estate auction next week.

   _____

2. Neither Mary nor Sarah have replied to our invitation.

   _____

3. The reason for his actions have never been clear.

   _____

4. The tour group are leaving the hotel at nine o'clock this morning.

   _____

5. The rooms in the old house are small and gloomy.

   _____

6. The number of tickets to be sold on the dream home have been set at 3999.

   _____

7. Here are the last two pieces of the puzzle.

   _____

8. Any one of the salespeople are willing to assist you.

   _____

9. Rachel finds that a calm disposition and infinite patience is important on her job.

   _____

10. I can't understand why either of you want to paint the trim on the house.

   _____

11. The department head, in conjunction with three members of his staff, has worked very hard to make the conference a success.

_____

12. The most interesting part of his latest novel is the design on the front cover.

_____

13. Measles are catching.

_____

14. A dental plan and group life insurance is part of the company's benefits package.

_____

15. Mike, like all his brothers, seem to be very outspoken.

_____

16. Lynne's family have lived in Québec, New Brunswick, and Saskatchewan.

_____

17. One benefit of these aerobic exercises are improved muscle tone.

_____

18. Fear of falling and fear of loud noises is instinctive.

_____

19. Neither the director nor the actors is pleased with the reviews.

_____

20. The criteria for selecting scholarship winners is very stringent.

_____

Review Exercise 8: General Review of Verbs

Correct any errors in the use of verbs. Revise sentences in which the passive voice is unnecessary. Put C beside a correct sentence.

1. I answered the phone after it had rang for what seemed to have been an eternity.

   _____

2. I should of let it keep ringing.

   _____

3. A bunch of words were rattled off in a dull, distant voice.

   _____

4. I hanged up the phone and laid in my bed, trying not to think.

   _____

5. I couldn't find it in me to go back to sleep, to cry, or even to care.

   _____

6. Finally I climbed out of bed and my clothes were put on.

   _____

7. When I stepped outside, the morning light dancing around my car.

   _____

8. As the keys to the car was ripped from my pocket, I thought about how much I wanted to drive it, and throwed my keys as far as I could.

   _____

9. I walked down the street intent on not caring—not caring about where I was going, where my keys was, or what the dull, distant voice had said.

   _____

10. I tried to ignore the cold morning wind, but my body shivered and my hands were numb.

    _____

11. With a sigh of defeat and despair my coat was buttoned up.

_____

12. If I would have been James Dean in a movie, I wouldn't have cared about the cold.

_____

13. Cars was filing past me like an army marching off to war.

_____

14. I began to wish I had drove my car so that I could loose myself in the flow of infinite traffic.

_____

15. My legs had began to tire, so I catched a bus.

_____

16. Suddenly I was horrified by the thought of being trapped on a bus.

_____

17. As I swang my eyes across the passengers, I seen them all staring at me.

_____

18. I spent the rest of the bus ride trying to decide if James Dean use to care but didn't show it or if he was too scared to care.

_____

19. Just before the bridge I hopped off the bus, climbed over the railing, and wondered what would happen if I dove off.

_____

20. While I was calculating that there were fifty metres to the water, my thoughts were lead in another direction: Would I ever find my car keys?

_____

Correcting Errors in Pronoun Agreement 1: Identifying the Antecedent

A **pronoun** is a word that is used in place of a noun. Usually the pronoun substitutes for a noun that has been stated earlier. The noun to which the pronoun refers is called its **antecedent**.

> My father has finally finished the deck. Now he plans to replace the old kitchen cabinets. [*He* is the pronoun that refers to the antecedent *father*.]

Singular nouns should be matched with **singular pronouns** and **plural nouns** should be matched with **plural pronouns**. Most of the time this is quite easy to do.

> **Ms. Allen** is in conference. **She** has asked not to be disturbed.
> **The clothes** are in the dryer. Please take **them** out when the cycle is finished.

Problem: Identifying the Antecedent in Sentences with Prepositional Phrases

Sometimes the pronoun and the antecedent are separated by a prepositional phrase. Watch for sentences in which the subject is followed by a phrase such as *of the children, of the workers, of the students, of the members.*

In the following sentence, *shortage* is the antecedent of the pronoun. Because *shortage* is singular, the pronoun following it should be singular.

NOT   The shortage of food and water is making (their) impact. *wrong*

BUT   The **shortage** of food and water is making **its** impact.

In other sentences the noun may be followed by a phrase beginning with *including, along with,* or *as well as.* Treat these phrases as prepositional phrases.

NOT   Mrs. Ho, along with all the family members, expressed their appreciation to the minister.

BUT   **Mrs. Ho**, along with all the family members, expressed **her** appreciation to the minister.

In this sentence, *Mrs. Ho* is the antecedent. *Mrs. Ho* is singular, so the pronoun referring to it should be singular.

Revision Strategies

1. Identify prepositional phrases by enclosing them in parentheses.
2. Remember that the antecedent of the pronoun is **not** located in the prepositional phrase.
3. Match a singular pronoun with a singular antecedent and a plural pronoun with a plural antecedent.

Exercise 1

Correct all errors in pronoun agreement in the following sentences. Put C beside a correct sentence.

1. The chairman, along with all the board members, has made their position on this issue well known.

   _____

2. The problems involved in even starting this project are numerous. It can, however, be overcome.

   _____

3. Each of the careers described in this handbook has its own rewards.

   _____C_____

4. The colours in this fabric have lost its original brightness.

   _____

5. The chief administrator, including all the members of her staff, expressed their satisfaction.

Correcting Errors in Pronoun Agreement 2: Indefinite Pronouns

Problem

Indefinite pronouns are often not matched correctly with other pronouns.

NOT   **Everybody** must hand in **their** paper before the final bell.

BUT   **Everybody** must hand in **his or her** paper before the final bell.

Revision Strategies

1. Remember that the following indefinite pronouns are singular and should be matched with singular pronouns and verbs:

anybody	everybody	somebody	nobody	neither
anything	everything	something	nothing	either
anyone	everyone	someone	no one (one)	each

Use the appropriate form of *his or her* in single sentences when you want to avoid using masculine pronouns to refer to both men and women, but do not use *he or she, him or her* repeatedly. Never use *he/she* or *s/he*.

Anybody interested in this course should leave **his or her** name with the secretary.
or
People interested in this course should leave **their** names with the secretary.

Watch for sentences in which the indefinite pronoun is separated from its antecedent by a prepositional phrase.

Neither of the men could make **his** position clear.

2. Some indefinite pronouns—such as *many, few, several*, and *both*—are almost always plural and take plural pronouns.

Many of the students in the self-paced math course have already completed all **their** assignments and quizzes.
A few have yet to write **their** final exams.

3. The indefinite pronouns *all*, *some*, and *none* can be singular or plural. These pronouns are often followed by prepositional phrases. The noun in the prepositional phrase determines whether the indefinite pronoun is singular or plural.

> None of the <u>**tools**</u> have been put back in **their** proper places.
> [*Tools* is the antecedent of *their*.]
> All of the **money** has been returned to **its** rightful owner.
> [*Money* is the antecedent of *its*.]

Exercise 2

Correct all errors in pronoun agreement in the following sentences. Put C beside a correct sentence.

1. Everybody involved in this project wants to have their name included in the final report.

   _____

2. None of the team members wanted to share their rooms.

   C _____

3. All of the participants are eligible to enter their names in the draw for the trip to Barbados.

   _____

4. Nobody working for this company feels that their job is secure.

   _____

5. Some of the furniture has been moved from its usual place.

   _____

6. If anyone submits their paper early, the instructor will read the assignment and suggest revisions.

   _____

7. No one is allowed to leave their seat during the takeoff and landing.

   _____

8. Some of the silverware has lost its lustre.

   _____

9. Neither of the hiking parties has reached their destination.

_____

10. Someone or something put their bony fingers on my shoulders as I entered the darkened room.

_____

Correcting Errors in Pronoun Agreement 3: Pronouns Referring to Types of People

Problem

Many pronoun agreement errors occur because a singular noun referring to a type of person (the child, the teacher, the teenager, the drug addict, the impaired driver) is matched with a plural pronoun. The result is this kind of sentence:

> A new child in a day care centre will probably miss their mother.

Revision Strategies

You can avoid this error in three ways.

1. Use *his or her* instead of *their*.
2. Make the subject of the sentence plural.

> New children in a day care centre will probably miss their mothers.

3. Alternate masculine and feminine pronouns. If you are writing a paper on alcoholism, for instance, you can refer to the alcoholic as *he* in one paragraph and as *she* in the next. Do not alternate masculine and feminine pronouns sentence by sentence.

Exercise 3

Revise the following sentences to eliminate errors in pronoun agreement. Put C beside a correct sentence.

1. The single parent needs more flexibility in arranging their class timetables.

2. An effective administrator maintains good relations with all their staff members.

_____

3. The floundering first-year student needs to be encouraged to contact their instructors for extra help.

_____

4. Impaired drivers will now have a Denver boot attached to their vehicles.

_____C_____

5. The depressed teenager is often unwilling to reveal their problems to their parents or teacher.

_____

Correcting Errors in Pronoun Agreement 4: Collective Nouns

Problem

Collective nouns such as *committee, family, community, jury, band, group, herd,* and *flock* sometimes cause problems. When these nouns refer to people or animals acting as a single unit, they are considered singular and take singular pronouns.

The **committee** agreed to postpone **its** next meeting.

When these nouns refer to people acting as individuals, they are considered plural and take plural pronouns.

The **jury** were warned not to discuss the case with **their** families.

Exercise 4

Correct all errors in pronoun agreement. Write *C* beside a correct sentence.

1. The team has just finished their seventh straight road game.

_____

2. The dinner theatre audience ordered its drinks during intermission.

_____

3. The band have packed their instruments and are ready to leave.

_____

4. The dance committee presented their proposals to the student council executive.

_____

5. The stolen property has been returned to their owner.

_____

Correcting Errors in Pronoun Agreement 5: *Either/Or* and *Neither/Nor* Sentences

Problem

When two singular nouns are joined with *and*, they are considered plural and take a plural pronoun.

> **Tom and Martha** are unwilling to consider sharing **their** money. [*Tom and Martha* is the antecedent of *their*.]

If you want to suggest that Tom and Martha are acting independently, you might write a sentence like this:

> Neither Tom nor Martha are willing to consider sharing their money.

The error here is that *Tom* and *Martha* are separate singular subjects and should be followed by a singular verb and a singular pronoun.

> **Neither Tom nor Martha is** willing to consider sharing **his or her** money.

Revision Strategies

1. In sentences where singular subjects are joined by *or, either/or, neither/nor,* use a singular pronoun and a singular verb.

Neither Bill nor Tom was prepared for questions **he was** asked.

2. When these conjunctions join a singular and a plural subject, put the plural subject last and make the following pronoun plural.

   Neither the teacher nor the students were pleased with **their** new computers.

Exercise 5

Correct all errors in pronoun agreement. Put C beside a correct sentence.

1. Either Karl or Ramon will give us their expert advice.

    ~~Karl or Ramon~~ *Ramon HIS*

2. If you can't find a copy of the book in the library, Sharon or Marlene will lend you hers.

   C

3. Neither the patients nor the doctor felt that their needs were being considered by the government.

4. Either Lydia or Katrina will present their views on abortion at this week's meeting of the philosophy forum.

5. Alex or Peter will drive their car in the demolition derby.

Correcting Errors in Pronoun Agreement 6: *Who, Which, That*

Problem

Sometimes *who, which,* and *that* act as antecedents for other pronouns. *Who, which,* and *that* may be singular or plural depending on whether their antecedents are singular or plural.

Errors in pronoun agreement occur when the pronoun following *who, which,* or *that* does not match the antecedent of these pronouns.

She is the kind of **person who** is never rude to **their** parents.

In this sentence the singular noun *person* is the antecedent of *who*, so *who* is singular and should be followed by a singular pronoun.

She is the kind of **person who** is never rude to **her** parents.

Revision Strategies

1. Look for the antecedent of *who, which,* or *that.* It will be the closest noun to these pronouns.
2. Make the pronoun following *who, which,* or *that* singular if the antecedent is singular; make the pronoun plural if the antecedent to *who, which,* or *that* is plural.

> The **group that** failed in **its** last attempt to climb Mount Everest has now disbanded. [*Group* is singular, so *that* is singular and takes the singular pronoun *its.*]
> The **people who** moved next door keep **their** three dogs penned in the back yard. [*People* is plural, so *who* is plural and takes the plural pronoun *their.*]

Exercise 6

Underline the antecedent of *who, which,* or *that* in each of the following sentences. Then correct all errors in pronoun agreement. Put *C* beside a correct sentence.

1. Anyone who wins a lottery must allow their name to be published in the newspaper.

   _____

2. A person who thinks this is a good place to eat must be out of their mind.

   _____

3. Every customer who purchases an appliance this weekend may enter their name in the draw for a trip to Hawaii.

   _____

4. The course on consumers and environmental waste, which was scheduled to have its first meeting on Tuesday, is attracting considerable interest.

   _____

5. The dog that is wandering the neighbourhood can't seem to find their way home.

   _____

6. He is one of those people who always think they are right.

   _____

7. A child who feels that their needs are usually met does not constantly seek attention.

   _____

8. Marvin is the person I told you about who washes their car every Sunday afternoon.

   _____

9. A single woman who lives in a basement apartment should keep their drapes drawn.

   _____

10. The people who belong to that church refuse to send their children to public schools.

    _____

Correcting Errors in Pronoun Agreement 7: Using Reflexive and Intensive Pronouns

Reflexive and intensive pronouns end in *self* and *selves*:

Singular	**Plural**
myself	ourselves
yourself	yourselves
himself/herself/itself/oneself	themselves

These pronouns are said to be **reflexive** when they refer to a subject that is acting upon itself:

Gina **burned herself** on the hot iron.

They are called **intensive pronouns** when they emphasize the noun they refer to:

The **president herself** will give the opening address.

Problem

There are two common errors in agreement between reflexive and intensive pronouns and their antecedents.

1. Plural forms are used incorrectly with singular antecedents.

NOT	Anyone who wants a second serving may help themselves.
CORRECT	Anyone who wants a second serving may help himself or herself.
BETTER	Those who want a second serving may help themselves.

2. Nonstandard forms such as *hisself, theirselves,* and *themself* are used.

NOT	Tom helped hisself to a second serving.
BUT	Tom helped himself to a second serving.
NOT	Sarah and Arnold hurt themself when they fell off their tandem bicycle.
BUT	Sarah and Arnold hurt themselves when they fell off their tandem bicycle.

Revision Strategies

1. Check to see whether the antecedent of a reflexive or intensive pronoun is singular or plural. Be sure that the pronoun matches its antecedent.
2. Use *self* with singular pronouns and *selves* with plural pronouns. Do not attach *self* (or *selves*) to *his* and *their*.

Exercise 7

Correct all errors in pronoun agreement. Put C beside a correct sentence.

1. Martin and Kevin have only themself to blame for their predicament.

_____

2. I want you to do all of the work yourself, Alexis.

_____

3. Someone has cut themselves on the broken glass.

4. The restaurant manager hisself is waiting on tables this evening.

_____

5. Elizabeth and Katrina bought tickets for us and for theirselves.

_____

Exercise 8: Pronoun Agreement

Correct all errors in pronoun agreement in the following sentences. Put *C* beside a correct sentence. Don't forget to make verbs singular or plural as necessary.

1. Every society has their legends about how people and animals were created.

_____

2. Stories about the creation of other races are often rather unflattering about it.

_____

3. In one Inuit version, a handsome young man, who wears a necklace with two large canine teeth around their neck, enters a family igloo during a violent blizzard.

_____

4. Neither the father nor the other members of the family are suspicious of the guest, so everyone invites him to share their portion of the evening meal.

_____

5. The next morning the young man has disappeared; each member of the family has their own idea about the situation.

_____

6. The father sees only animal tracks outside and decides it must have been made by the lead dog, who had come in disguised as a man.

_____

7. When his daughter becomes pregnant, the father paddles her out to an island in his kayak and they abandon her there.

_____

8. Night after night one of the dogs swims out to the island, taking his large, tender pieces of meat to the abandoned girl.

_____

9. Finally a large brood of children makes their appearance: three of them are Inuit, but three have big ears and noses like snouts.

_____

10. According to the legend, every white person and Indian has one of those three dog children among their ancestors.

_____

Review Exercise 9: Pronoun Agreement

Correct all errors in pronoun agreement. Write C beside a correct sentence.

1. Every person I've asked said they would have done exactly the same thing.

_____

2. Each applicant for the job will be judged on their own merit.

_____

3. The jury has reached their decision.

_____

4. If your piece of pie isn't large enough, Brett or Steve will share theirs with you.

_____

5. Bill says that either Doug or he will bring their truck to help you move.

_____

6. He is not someone who easily changes their mind.

_____

7. The tour group reached its hotel an hour earlier than expected.

_____

8. Some of the doors were torn from its hinges during the storm.

_____

9. Stella or Mary can tell you themselves what happened.

_____

10. The young man who cut the grass left their jacket on the rosebush.

_____

11. Only people who eat all their turnips will get dessert.

_____

12. Neither of the women has filed their income tax return yet.

_____

13. Nobody has submitted their name to serve on the grievance committee.

_____

14. Mrs. Hrychuk, along with the rest of the committee, wishes to convey her sincere apology for any inconvenience.

_____

15. The shortage of skilled labourers is beginning to have their consequences.

_____

16. Everybody who wants to give their opinion on this issue should contact the section head.

_____

17. Several members of the group wish to express their appreciation.

_____

18. None of the class, including the best students, wished to present their complaints directly to the principal.

_____

19. Linda or Debby must have put the money in their suitcase.

_____

20. The people who bought stock in this company have only theirself to blame.

_____

Correcting Errors in Pronoun Case

Pronouns change form depending on the ways they are used in a sentence. In English there are three pronoun cases: **subject, object,** and **possessive.**

Subject Case		Object Case		Possessive Case	
Singular	*Plural*	*Singular*	*Plural*	*Singular*	*Plural*
I	we	me	us	my/mine	our/ours
you	you	you	you	your/yours	your/yours
he	they	him	them	his	their/theirs
she		her		her/hers	
it		it		its	
who	who	whom	whom	whose	whose

Problem: Confusing Subject and Object Pronouns

You can see examples of common mistakes with subject, object, and possessive pronouns in these sentences:

Beth and **him** want to eat lunch now. [should be *Beth and he*]
You can leave the message with either my sister or **I.**
[should be *my sister or me*]
The dog wrapped **it's** leash around a tree. [should be *its*]

For most people, the main problem in choosing the correct pronoun case (subject, object, or possessive) involves recognizing when a pronoun is functioning in one of these three ways.

Basic Rules for Using Subject Pronouns

1. Use subject pronouns as the **subject** of a sentence or a clause.

We are going to a movie tonight.

- Don't be confused by compound subjects.

NOT   Elaine and *me* enjoyed our visit to Vancouver.

BUT   Elaine and *I* enjoyed our visit to Vancouver.

One way to avoid this confusion of subject and object pronouns is to use the pronoun alone in the sentence. You can see immediately that *Me enjoyed our visit* is incorrect and that *I* is the correct form.

- Don't be confused by subjects followed by an explanatory word or phrase.

NOT   **Us** homeowners are concerned about the increased traffic in the neighbourhood.

BUT   **We** homeowners are concerned about increased traffic in the neighbourhood.

- Don't be confused when the pronoun is part of an explanatory phrase following the subject.

NOT   The two of us—Cliff and **me**—decided to go into business together.

BUT   The two of us—Cliff and **I**—decided to go into business together.

2. Use subject pronouns after comparisons using *than* or *as*.

NOT   No one is more upset about this subject than **her**.

BUT   No one is more upset about this subject than **she**.

NOT   I am not as good a swimmer as **him**.

BUT   I am not as good a swimmer as **he**.

In these sentences, *than she* and *as he* are actually subordinate clauses from which the verb has been omitted. Putting the verb in helps to show that the pronoun is the subject of a clause and should be in the subject case.

Damien is as eager to join the club as **we** (are).
You are almost as tall as **I** (am).

3. Use subject pronouns after forms of the verb *to be*.
In spoken English, we often hear such constructions as *It's me* and *That's him at the door now*. In formal, written English, however, it's preferable to use subject pronouns after the verb to be.

It was **he** who told you that ridiculous story.
It is **she** who must accept responsibility.
That is my grandparents and **I** in the photograph.

4. Use *who* as a subject pronoun and *whom* as an object pronoun.

NOT   She is a specialist **whom** I am sure needs no introduction.

BUT   She is a specialist **who** I am sure need no introduction.

Note: Do not use reflexive pronouns as substitutes for personal pronouns.

NOT   My husband and **myself** are planning a trip to the Caribbean.

BUT   My husband and **I** are planning a trip to the Caribbean.

Exercise 1: Using Subject Pronouns Correctly

Correct the errors in pronoun case in the following sentences. Write C beside a correct sentence.

1. Us nonsmokers are petitioning to have the entire office building declared "smoke free."

   _____

2. Few people are as thoughtful and considerate as her.

   _____

3. Marilyn and him will be stopping at Niagara Falls on their way to Toronto.

   _____

4. Luigi said that his wife and him would be glad to spend Christmas with us.

   _____

5. It is they whom are indebted to us, not we who are indebted to them.

   _____

6. Carla decided that the three of them—David, Ricardo, and she—would spend the weekend fishing at the lake.

   _____

7. Hilda is upset that she had to cancel the trip because her grandmother and herself had been planning it for months.

   _____

8. Him and I had never been to the Maritimes until this year.

9. The winners are Michael, Joey, and me.

---

10. Jennifer is always intimidated by people older than her.

Basic Rules for Using Object Pronouns

1. Use object pronouns in compound objects after verbs and prepositions.

NOT Elizabeth told Sarah and **I** the truth about what **happened last** night.

BUT Elizabeth told Sarah and **me** the truth about what happened last night.

NOT Ernest claims he sent the cheque to Lydia and **she** last week.

BUT Ernest claims he sent the cheque to Lydia and **her** last week.

As a test, use the pronoun alone as the object of the verb or preposition, as in *Elizabeth told me* and *Ernest sent the cheque to her*. This technique will help you to avoid substituting subject pronouns for object pronouns.

2. Use **whom** as the object of a verb or a preposition, as in these examples:

Are you the person **to whom** I was speaking yesterday? [*Whom* is the object of the preposition *to*.]

About whom are you speaking? [*Whom* is the object of the preposition *about*.]

She is a person **whom** we all admire and respect. [*Whom* is the object of the verbs *respect* and *admire*.]

Whom do you believe? [*Whom* is the object of the verb *believe*.]

3. Do not use reflexive pronouns as substitutes for object pronouns.

NOT Please call Lester or **myself** regarding the new contract.

BUT Please call Lester or **me** regarding the new contract.

Exercise 2: Using Object Pronouns Correctly

Correct the errors in pronoun case in the following sentences. Write *C* beside a correct sentence.

1. Leonard argued that it was unfair to place all the blame for the mishap on Howard and himself.

---

2. Paul suddenly turned away from Anne and started talking to Philip and I.

_____

3. This change in policy concerns me and the people with who I share it.

_____

4. About four o'clock in the morning the police caught up with my friends and I.

_____

5. Cheryl didn't recognize Marco or he until they had walked right by her.

_____

6. Please return the lecture notes to either me or her by the end of the week.

_____

7. Have you told Andreas and she the good news yet?

_____

8. Whom can we credit with this unique achievement?

_____

9. Let's keep this matter between you and I.

_____

10. They live across the street from my parents and myself.

_____

Basic Rules for Using Possessive Pronouns

1. The possessive pronouns *yours, his, hers, its, ours,* and *theirs* do not take apostrophes.

    NOT   Is that book on the table **your's**?
    BUT   Is that book on the table **yours**?

2. Indefinite pronouns do take apostrophes to show possession.

    Somebody's book is on the table.

3. Be careful not to confuse the possessive form *its* with the contraction *it's* [*it is*]. **Never** use *its'*.

POSSESSIVE	The parrot sat on **its** perch.
CONTRACTION	**It's** not unusual for a parrot to live over fifty years.

4. Don't confuse the possessive *whose* with the contraction *who's* [*who is*].

POSSESSIVE	**Whose** gloves are these?
CONTRACTION	I'm not sure **who's** to blame for this mess.

Exercise 3: Using *Its* and *Whose* Correctly

Insert *its* or *it's* and *whose* or *who's* in the following sentences.

1. My dog chased _____ tail.
2. _____ going to tell Don that Dad has just driven over his skateboard?
3. _____ difficult to say just what he will do.
4. Students _____ last names begin with A will register tomorrow morning.
5. I'm afraid my old car has driven _____ last kilometre.
6. _____ problem is this, anyway?
7. _____ too late now.
8. _____ going out with the student driver today?
9. The cover for this book seriously mispresents _____ content.
10. Is this the person _____ supposed to represent us?

Exercise 4: Using Possessive Pronouns Correctly

Correct all errors with possessive pronouns in the following sentences. Write C beside a correct sentence.

1. Its a dog-eat-dog world out there.

_____

2. Whose gloves are these?

_____

3. Everyones paper has been graded.

_____

4. Every dog must have it's day.

_____

5. People who's homes were destroyed in the flood will receive government assistance.

_____

6. Who's holding down the fort?

_____

7. Ones good name should be ones most important possession.

_____

8. The notes thrown in the wastepaper basket are hers.

_____

9. Have the police determined who's fingerprints were on the murder weapon?

_____

10. The deer stopped and turned its head towards the approaching hunters.

_____

Exercise 5: Pronoun Case

Correct all errors in pronoun case in the following sentences. Put C beside a correct sentence.

1. Lenore said that Martha and her will be at the library until eight this evening.

_____

2. The house key is not in it's usual place.

_____

3. He is a man who we would all agree needs no introduction.

_____

4. You will be hearing from Bertha or I within two days.

_____

5. Darryl may be the shortest player on the team, but no one is faster than him.

   _____

6. George and myself are planning to go the beach this Sunday.

   _____

7. The three of us—Brian, Christine, and me—are being interviewed for a television news report.

   _____

8. Whose life is it anyway?

   _____

9. Mr. Cheng spoke to Kevin and she about summer jobs.

   _____

10. Melody could see that Esther was as determined as she.

    _____

11. The manager wants all applications sent to herself after they have been screened by the personnel department.

    _____

12. The wolf withdrew into it's den.

    _____

13. Someones wallet is lying in the street.

    _____

14. The bear ambled through the woods, minding its own business.

    _____

15. In May, us business students will be attending a career day at the community college

    _____

Correcting Errors in Pronoun Reference

Problem

Errors in pronoun reference occur when you use a pronoun that does not refer clearly to a specific noun.

> When I worked in retail, I dealt with both very pleasant customers and very obnoxious ones, which made me decide not to pursue a career in that field.
>
> They say that disposable diapers are a serious pollution problem.

These sentences are unclear because they use pronouns that do not refer to specific antecedents. In the first sentence, *which* seems to refer to the idea of dealing with both pleasant and obnoxious customers, but dealing with pleasant customers wouldn't be a deterrent to working in retail. In the second sentence *they* might refer to people in general, environmental advocates, or the manufacturers of cloth diapers.

Basic Rule

The basic rule of pronoun reference is that every pronoun you use should clearly and logically refer to the closest preceding noun that could be its antecedent. When you are checking for errors in pronoun reference in your own writing, look for pronouns that do not have a specific antecedent. Pay special attention to the following:

Vague Uses of *They* and *It*

1. Be careful not to use *they* to refer to people in general.

> **They** say the poverty in Haiti is appalling.

Who are *they*? tourists? government officials? your next door neighbours? A clearer version of this sentence would read:

> Canadian tourists say the poverty in Haiti is appalling.

2. Avoid sentences with two uses of *it*.

> **It** soon became obvious that **it** was completely out of control.

This sentence would be confusing even if the preceding sentence made clear what was out of control. A clearer sentence would read:

It soon became obvious that inflation was out of control.

3. Avoid sentences in which an implied antecedent substitutes for a stated antecedent.

When Graham phoned the garage, **they** said the car would be ready by noon.

We are left to assume that the mechanic or the service attendant provided this information. The revised sentence might read like this:

When Graham phoned the garage, the mechanic said the car would be ready by noon.

You can see a similar problem in the use of *it* in this sentence:

After I checked on the admission requirements, I saw that it wouldn't be a problem.

We assume that acceptance would not be a problem, but the revised sentence makes this clear:

After I checked on the admission requirements, I saw that my acceptance wouldn't be a problem.

Vague Uses of *This, That,* and *Which*

1. In everyday speech we often say *That's terrible,* or *This is great news!* Even though *that* and *this* refer to a whole set of circumstances, our listeners can usually figure out what we mean. In writing, however, sentences where *this, that,* and *which* refer to an entire preceding sentence or clause can be confusing—especially if these pronouns refer to sentences or clauses expressing more than one idea.

Grandmother MacLeod tells Vanessa that God loves order, but Vanessa sees that life around her is often in disarray, and **this** confuses her.

In this sentence, the nearest noun to *this* is *disarray*, but Vanessa is not confused by disarray. She is confused by the contradiction between her own experience and her grandmother's pronouncements. The revised sentence makes this point more clearly:

Vanessa is confused by the contradiction between the disarray of life around her and her grandmother's statement that God loves order.

2. The following sentence presents a similar problem with the use of *which*.

> Melissa had a flat tire and was caught in rush hour traffic, **which** made her late.

Here the antecedent for *which* is *traffic*, but both the flat tire and the rush hour traffic made Melissa late. The revised sentence is clearer and more direct:

> Melissa was late because she had a flat tire and was caught in rush hour traffic.

3. In the next example, the vague use of *that* creates a problem.

> I wanted to go to a movie, but I had to study for an exam, and **that's** why I was grouchy.

The revised version of this sentence states the reason for the writer's grouchiness more clearly:

> I was grouchy because I wanted to go to a movie, but I had to study for an exam.

Sentences with Too Many Antecedents

Sometimes a pronoun seems to refer to more than one antecedent in a sentence. This problem often occurs in sentences that contain indirect speech.

> When Dino told Len that he had won a scholarship, he was very excited.

Because *he* in both parts of this sentence could refer to either Dino or Len, we don't know who won the scholarship or who was excited. The simplest way to revise this kind of sentence is to put part of it into direct speech:

> Dino was excited when he told Len, "I've won a scholarship."

Or you could revise the sentence like this:

> Dino, who had won a scholarship, was very excited when he told Len the news.

Exercise

Revise the following sentences to eliminate unclear pronoun reference.

1. Karl told Edward that he would run the company one day.

2. Trudy had a bad cold and a strained muscle, but that didn't stop her from running in the race.

_____

3. Although Mr. Lincoln regarded himself as an intelligent and flexible person, they told him that he was too old to begin a new career.

_____

4. Costs have risen and profits have declined, which is why the company must lay off fifty employees.

_____

5. When Peter contacted the telephone company, they said they would send a repair person the next day.

_____

6. I used to have trouble sticking with it, but now that I'm attending AA meetings regularly, it's much easier.

_____

7. A job in a bush camp involves long hours, demanding working conditions, and long stretches of isolation, which is why it doesn't attract many people.

_____

8. Twenty train cars were derailed, but no one was injured in it.

_____

9. The computer literacy course is extremely useful but hard to get into, and this discouraged Maria.

_____

10. When the doctor phoned the cardiac ICU to check for space, they said that nothing was available.

_____

Maintaining a Consistent Point of View: Avoiding Pronoun Shifts

Problem

Abrupt shifts from the expected personal pronoun change a reader's point of view and can be very disconcerting.

> The novice **driver** is especially likely to become rattled when **you** experience rush hour traffic for the first time.

	Subject Pronouns		Object Pronouns	
	Singular	Plural	Singular	Plural
1st person	I	we	me	us
2nd person	you	you	you	you
3rd person	he, she	they	him, her	them
	it, one		it, one	

Basic Rule

The basic rule here is to use first or second or third person pronouns **consistently** throughout a piece of writing. You could revise the example above by using either *you* or *he or she*.

> As a novice driver, **you** are especially likely to become rattled when **you** experience rush hour traffic for the first time.
> The novice **driver** is especially likely to become rattled when **he or she** experiences rush hour traffic for the first time.

Exercise

Revise the following paragraph to correct shifts in point of view. You can change the person of the pronoun, or you can substitute an appropriate noun for the pronoun.

Planning to buy a new home involves a number of important decisions. Homebuyers can choose from a variety of housing types, including single family dwellings and multiple family dwellings, such a duplexes or townhomes. You must consider such requirements as proximity to work, schools, and shopping; the number of bedrooms and bathrooms; and the size of the yard. We must also decide whether to purchase an existing home or have one built. Many of your decisions will depend on your personal lifestyle and preferences, but they will depend even more on one's financial resources. It may be sobering for a person to realize that what I want in a home and what I can afford can be very far apart indeed.

Review Exercise 10: Pronoun Case, Reference, Shifts

Correct any errors in pronoun case, reference, and pronouns of address in the following sentences. Some sentences have more than one error.

1. In the second part of the Inuit creation legend, it tells us about the father going to the island for his daughter.

   _____

2. Him and his fellow boatmen rowed out to the island in an umiak, a large skin boat.

   _____

3. On their way back, a storm came up, which they were afraid would capsize the boat.

   _____

4. One of the boatmen suggested that the father and themselves should throw the daughter overboard, because it would lighten the load.

   _____

5. You couldn't imagine a more heartless father than him, for when she tried to climb back into the boat, he cut off her fingers. These became seals.

   _____

6. The next time she tried to climb into the boat, he cut off her hands and they became walruses.

   _____

7. Her and her father had one last confrontation when he cut off her forearms. This time they turned into whales.

   _____

8. Then the daughter disappeared into the depths, where she became Sedna, the half woman, half fish whom controls all the sea.

   _____

9. They sing many songs to this powerful goddess, which they hope will persuade her to send them good hunting.

_____

10. The Inuit tell this sort of creation story as a myth. One would not find the names of actual people in them.

_____

11

Adjectives and Adverbs

Practice with Troublesome Adjectives and Adverbs

Adjectives describe nouns, and **adverbs** describe verbs, adjectives, and other adverbs.

ADJECTIVES   The **big red** ball drifted out into the **stormy** lake. [*Big* and *red* describe the noun *ball*; *stormy* describes the noun *lake.*]

ADVERBS   The instructor speaks very quickly. [*Quickly* describes the verb *speaks*; *very* describes the adverb *quickly.*]

ADVERB   This sweater is **too** small. [*Too* is an adverb describing the adjective *small.*]

Problem Adjectives and Adverbs

There are a few adjectives and adverbs that are often used incorrectly. These include:

1. *Good* and *Well*

Good is an adjective; *well* is usually an adverb.

NOT   Bill **did good** on his French test.

BUT   Bill **did well** on his French test.

Note 1: You can use *well* as an adjective in reference to health.

After a bout of flu that lasted three weeks, the baby is finally **well.**

Note 2: You can use *good* after verbs of existence and sensation.

The cookies **smell good.**

I **feel good** after ten minutes in a sauna.

2. *Bad/Badly* and *Real/Really*

Bad and *real* are adjectives; *badly* and *really* are adverbs.

| NOT | I am **real glad** to see you. |
| BUT | I am **really glad** to see you. |

| NOT | He was **hurt bad** in the accident. |
| BUT | He was **hurt badly** in the accident. |

Note: *Bad* can be used as an adverb in informal usage after the verbs *feel* and *look*.

I **feel bad** about your car accident.
It **looks bad** for her to be out until 3:00 a.m.

You would rephrase these sentences, however, in more formal writing.

I **feel badly** (very sorry) about your car accident.
Staying out until 3:00 a.m. **may damage her reputation.**

3. *Less* and *Fewer*

Less is an adjective used to describe items that cannot be considered as separate objects: less snow, less milk, less bread, less trouble. *Fewer* is an adjective used to describe things that can be counted: fewer people, fewer problems, fewer quarts of milk, fewer loaves of bread.

| NOT | **Less people** came to the game than were expected. |
| BUT | **Fewer people** came to the game than were expected. |

4. *Hardly* and *Barely*

Do **not** use these adverbs in negative constructions.

| NOT | I **can't hardly** hear you. |
| BUT | I **can hardly** hear you. |

| NOT | We **don't barely** have enough time. |
| BUT | We **barely** have enough time. |

Degrees of Comparison

Both adjectives and adverbs have degrees of comparison.

POSITIVE	clean/fast
COMPARATIVE	cleaner/faster
SUPERLATIVE	cleanest/fastest

Use the **comparative** form to compare **two** things.

This glass is cleaner than that one.
He runs faster than his brother.

Use the **superlative** form to compare **three or more** things.

> This is the clean**est** glass in the house.
> He ran fast**est** in the final race.

Some adjectives add *er* and *est* endings to form the comparative and superlative degrees. Others, such as those ending in *ful* (useful), *less* (pointless), and *ing* (interesting), add *more* to form the comparative degree (more useful, more pointless, more interesting) and *most* to form the superlative degree (most useful, most pointless, most interesting). If you are not sure which form is correct, consult a dictionary.

Note: Do **not** use double comparatives or superlatives: *most cleanest*, *more faster*. Remember that some adjectives, such as *unique, perfect, empty*, do not have comparative or superlative degrees.

Exercise 1: Adjectives and Adverbs

Underline the correct word form in parentheses.

1. The mother walked (quiet/quietly) into the room to check on the sleeping baby.
2. That is the (worse/worst) movie I have ever seen.
3. The toaster works (good/well) now that you have repaired it.
4. Max is (less happy/less happier) living in an apartment than he was in a house.
5. How (bad/badly) will the budget cutbacks affect the personnel budget?
6. This exquisite vase is the (most beautiful/beautifullest) in the museum.
7. The judges had trouble choosing the winning entries at the food fair because all the dishes tasted (real/really) (good/well).
8. John and Howard are both hardworking, but John is the (more determined/most determined).
9. I (can't hardly/can hardly) understand a word she says.
10. This year (fewer/less) students have registered in the introductory Latin class.

Demonstratives

The **demonstrative** pronouns, *this, that, these, those*, can function as adjectives. *This* and *that* are singular; *these* and *those* are plural.

Do **not** use *these* or *those* with singular nouns.

NOT   **These kind** of food processors are more versatile than other machines.

BUT   **These kinds** of food processors. . . .

         or

         This kind of food processor. . . .

Do not use *them* as a demonstrative pronoun.

NOT   Please pass me **them books**.

BUT   Please pass me **those books**.

Noun-on-Noun Modifiers

In many expressions nouns can modify other nouns, as in school dance, government agency, furniture business. It's a good idea, however, to avoid noun-on-noun modifiers whenever the result is awkward or confusing.

NOT   science experiment

BUT   scientific experiment

NOT   technology achievement

BUT   technological achievement

Phrases and Clauses with *Like* and *As*

In this sentence, *like* is a preposition:

My love is **like** a red, red rose.

Use *as* (*as if, as though*) instead of *like* to introduce a subordinate clause that functions as an adverb.

NOT   She acts **like** she doesn't know us.

BUT   She acts **as if** she doesn't know us.

       or

       She acts **as though** she doesn't know us.

Exercise 2:

Correct all errors in the use of noun-on-noun modifiers, demonstrative pronouns, the use of *like* and *as* in the following sentences. Put C beside a correct sentence.

1. I've decided to increase my charity donations this year.

_____

2. Please put them flowers in a vase.

_____

3. Isadora dances like the wind.

174 _____

4. The administration costs for the project exceeded projections.

_____

5. It looks like it will snow tonight.

_____

Review Exercise 11: Adjectives and Adverbs

Correct any errors in the use of adjectives and adverbs in the following sentences. Put *C* beside a correct sentence.

1. My twin and I have the most unique relationship you can imagine.

_____

2. We're real good friends, but we don't hardly do anything without competing to see who is best.

_____

3. We take almost all the same courses, and we try to see who can get the most perfect grades.

_____

4. Sometimes I do well on an exam and my twin does badly.

_____

5. Sometimes my twin has less mistakes and I do really bad.

_____

6. We also compete to see who is bestest at sports.

_____

7. My twin generally wins less games of tennis, but I am the slowest skier.

_____

8. I am the better cook when it comes to desserts, but my twin's homemade bread tastes real well.

_____

9. You can't barely see any difference in our height or weight.

_____

10. But the first Saturday of every month we measure to see who has grown more taller and climb on the scales to see who has put on less kilos.

_____

Review Exercise 12: General Review of Grammar

Revise the following sentences so that verbs, pronouns, adjectives, and adverbs are used correctly. Some sentences contain more than one error. Put C beside a correct sentence.

1. Tim speaks so soft that I can't hardly hear what he is saying.

_____

2. You have shrank my brand new wool sweater.

_____

3. Joe's parents are as excited about the scholarship as him.

_____

4. Kevin says that Ms. Smith has assigned the new account to Doug and he.

_____

5. We would not of been able to finish the job on time without Nathan's help.

_____

6. Sandy received the bill in June, but it wasn't paid until the end of July.

_____

7. Between you and I, Pauline should get the lead in the play because she is a much better actress than Melanie.

_____

8. Someone has left their fountain pen on the instructor's desk.

_____

9. Hans has broke all swimming records at the local club.

_____

10. If Sonya would have asked me, I certainly would of given her a straight answer.

_____

11. Laurence, Dick, and him are going to the lake for the weekend.

_____

12. Neither Barbara nor Linda have registered for courses in the next term.

_____

13. Donald stood up so sudden that he became dizzy and almost lost his balance.

_____

14. The band have been booked to play both Friday and Saturday nights.

_____

15. There is only two copies of the text left in the bookstore.

_____

16. Neither the team manager nor the players' agents have proposed an agreement satisfactory to both sides.

_____

17. Bridget sewed the blouse so careless that it soon began to come apart at the seams.

_____

18. When I seen Louanne last week, she said that Debbie and her will be studying accounting at university in the fall.

_____

19. The children pushed open the door and run into the back yard.

_____

20. Nicholas is earning less money at his new job, but he is more happier with the work.

_____

21. Our team are playing good this year and will likely make the playoffs.

_____

22. Quick reflexes and good coordination is important to a goalie.

_____

23. The assistant manager thinks that either Connie or Maria have agreed to change their shift so that Patricia can have Sunday off.

_____

24. Cynthia owns the stereo system, but the record collection belong to both Clark and she.

_____

25. Anyone who parks in this No Parking zone will have their car towed away.

_____

26. A word to the wise being sufficient.

_____

27. The lead runner suddenly clasped their leg and fell to the ground in agony.

_____

28. The runner laid on the track, unable to rise.

_____

29. I can't find my garden shears, but here is the rake and the shovel.

_____

30. In Alberta there are less jobs in the oil industry now than there were in the 1970s.

_____

12
Punctuation
and Mechanics

Practice with Commas

Basic Rules for Using Commas with Clauses

1. Use a comma before a coordinate conjunction (*and, but, or, nor, for, yet, so*) to join main clauses.

   Someone had been rifling through the desk, but there was no sign of a forced entry.

   The comma can be omitted if the clauses are short and there is no danger of misreading.

   You hang the light fixture and I'll watch.

2. Use a comma after an introductory subordinate clause.

   Although Ned woke up with a high fever and a splitting headache, he put in a full day's work.

   Do **not** use a comma if the clause comes at the end of the sentence and is essential to its meaning.

   Rajiv went straight to his evening class after he had finished work.

   Use a comma if this clause is not closely related to the rest of the sentence.

   Susan felt apprehensive, although she didn't know why.

3. Use commas between three or more clauses in a series.

   We decided that Tom would drive, that Jim would navigate, and that I would sleep during the first leg of the trip.

4. Use either two commas or no commas around clauses beginning with *who, which,* and *that.*

Do **not** put commas around **restrictive** clauses. A restrictive clause provides information that is necessary to define the subject of the main clause. Clauses beginning with *that* are usually restrictive.

> The antique clock that is sitting on the mantel is a family heirloom.
> Homeowners who do not pay their property taxes by June 30 are subject to a penalty.

Put commas around **nonrestrictive** clauses. A nonrestrictive clause provides additional information. Nonrestrictive clauses often follow capitalized nouns. Clauses beginning with *which* are usually nonrestrictive.

> At the Gombe Stream Research Centre, which is on the shores of Lake Tanganyika, Jane Goodall has studied chimpanzees for over thirty years.
> Cynthia, who is a computer programmer, plans to begin graduate studies in computer applications this fall.

5. Put commas around parenthetical clauses that slightly interrupt the flow of the sentence.

> The essay, she suddenly remembered, was still sitting on the kitchen table.
> Housework, I must admit, can be a useful way of working off excess energy.

6. Use commas to set off clauses in quotation marks (direct speech) from the rest of the sentence.

> "I'm sure," said the spider to the fly, "that you will make a delightful companion."

7. Use a comma to set off a question that comes at the end of a sentence.

> You're going to the party, aren't you?

Exercise 1: Using Commas with Clauses

Add commas where necessary. Put C beside a sentence that does not require punctuation.

1. Darlene mailed all the invitations and Sharon arranged for the caterer and the band.

_____

2. If you want low prices and good merchandise shop at Big Spenders.

_____

3. The rest it seems to me is up to you.

_____

4. I haven't seen the movie yet although I hear it's very good.

_____

5. They were excited about the trip for they had never travelled to a foreign country.

_____

6. The eyes of the woman in the picture seemed to be following me as I walked across the room.

_____

7. He didn't know any of the correct answers nor could he think of how to fake his way through the exam.

_____

8. After the children ate the adults enjoyed a quiet dinner.

_____

9. "That sounds delicious" my companion replied "but I don't have any room for dessert."

_____

10. This is the site where we plan to build our cottage.

_____

11. Joseph had hoped to find the book in the library stacks but someone had already borrowed the only copy.

_____

12. As we stood watching the building began to collapse.

_____

13. You wash and I'll dry.

_____

14. Stella who is organizing the dance has scheduled a meeting for the people who have agreed to serve on the refreshment committee.

_____

15. Magnetic Hill which is located near Moncton is an optical illusion.

_____

16. Howard knew that he had made it in the company when he was given the key to the executive men's washroom.

_____

17. The mouse ran up the clock the clock struck one and the mouse ran down.

_____

18. The problem I realized was with the television set.

_____

19. The house that Jack built is tumbling down for lack of repairs.

_____

20. This is the spot where the treasure is supposed to be buried.

_____

Basic Rules for Using Commas with Words and Phrases

1. Put a comma after a mild interjection and after *yes* and *no* when they begin a sentence.

   Oh, I wouldn't worry about it if I were you.
   Yes, we do have that item in stock.

2. Put a comma after an introductory phrase longer than five words.

   While studying creative writing at college, Theresa wrote a short story titled "Life in the Slow Lane."

3. Put a comma after a short introductory phrase if you want to emphasize it or use it as a transition.

Fortunately, no one was injured in the accident.
For example, peonies are excellent perennials for this region.

Put a comma after *however* when it means "nevertheless." Do **not** use a comma when it means "by whatever means" or "to whatever extent."

However, be sure to arrive on time.
However you travel, arrive on time.

Commas with other conjunctive adverbs are optional. Short ones (*thus, then, therefore*) usually do not take a comma; longer ones (*nevertheless, consequently*) often do.

Therefore I declare the meeting adjourned.

Omit commas after most other short introductory phrases unless the comma helps to prevent misreading.

Hiding inside, the children tried to keep from giggling.

4. Use commas to separate three or more words or phrases in a series. Always use a comma before the last item.

Lillian's favourite lunch is celery and carrot sticks, soup and crackers, and cookies.

Do **not** use a comma after the last item when the series functions as the subject of the sentence.

Strawberries, raspberries, and blueberries are now in season.

Do **not** use a comma between two items joined with *and*.

It's very hot and humid today.

5. Use commas to separate a series of adjectives that could be joined with *and*.

She was a sensitive, quiet child.

Do **not** use commas between adjectives that could not be joined with *and*.

He gave her a beautiful red rose.

6. Put commas around nonrestrictive phrases.

The two cougars, sleeping peacefully in their cage, looked as harmless as house cats.
Fred Goldschmidt, manager of a local book store, and Sharon Young, managing director of an engineering firm, have been invited to speak at the business seminar.

7. Put commas around interjections and parenthetical expressions.

I'll take, oh, half a dozen doughnuts.
You are, as a matter of fact, quite wrong.

8. Put commas around nouns of address.

This message, Keith, is for you.

9. Use a comma to set off a contrasting element that comes at the end of the sentence.

I ordered coffee, not tea.

10. Use a comma to separate the day of the month from the year.

William Wordsworth was born April 7, 1770.

The comma is optional when only the month and year are given.

William Wordsworth was born in April 1770.

Use a comma after the year when the date comes in the middle of a sentence.

William Wordsworth was born April 7, 1770, and died April 23, 1850.

11. Use a comma with geographic names and addresses.

Leninakan, Armenia, was devastated in a terrible earthquake.

12. Put a comma after the salutation in personal letters and after the closing in all letters.

Dear Aunt Judith,
Yours truly,

Exercise 2: Using Commas with Words and Phrases

Add commas where necessary. Write *C* beside a sentence that does not require punctuation.

1. In our history class we are studying the Renaissance the great revival of learning that marked the transition from the medieval to the modern world.

---

2. Wearing a heavy parka and mukluks Murray felt decidedly out of place when he got off the plane in Vancouver.

---

3. No Clarence hasn't arrived at the office yet.

_____

4. However I'll have him call you when he gets in.

_____

5. The volunteer emergency services organization requires bedding shoes clothing and canned goods.

_____

6. The platypus is indigenous to Australia not South America.

_____

7. Above the stars looked like diamonds.

_____

8. Moving quietly in order not to wake the baby Mrs. Bigelow straightened the blankets.

_____

9. Then she tiptoed from the room and closed the door.

_____

10. Chantilly a delicate lace is named after the town in northern France where it is made.

_____

11. The family moved to Fergus Ontario on July 1 1967.

_____

12. We hope Mr. Ventura that you will list your home with our professional real estate firm.

_____

13. The Sartorial Emporium now closed for renovations will reopen on September 1.

_____

14. Sir Frederick Banting the co-discoverer of insulin received the Nobel Prize for medicine in 1923.

_____

15. Wapiti for example are often seen in the park.

_____

16. Ron was the only person able to solve the complex intricate puzzle.

_____

17. The man carrying the briefcase is the instructor.

_____

18. The cheque as a matter of fact is in the mail.

_____

19. Before building a fence more than two metres high you must apply to the city for a building permit.

_____

20. There is a large yellow ribbon tied around the old oak tree.

_____

Exercise 3

Add commas where necessary. Write C beside a sentence that does not require punctuation.

1. Stopping abruptly Wendy realized that she had left her purse in the airport washroom.

_____

2. Witches ghosts and goblins wander the streets on Halloween which falls each year on October 31.

_____

3. When we went to buy tickets we were faced with a two-block line-up.

_____

4. However we decided to put up with the wait because we were determined to see the concert.

   _____

5. George did not get the job because he was late for the interview he was unshaven and unkempt and he complained constantly about his previous employer.

   _____

6. After the severe windstorm had finally subsided the community surveyed the damage.

   _____

7. Howard was worried that he would not receive the letter in time but it arrived before the mail strike began.

   _____

8. Charlotte baked a cake and Betty made several batches of cookies.

   _____

9. I thought that the Wilsons were vacationing in the Cook Islands not the Society Islands.

   _____

10. Barbara has to paint the fence repair the leaky faucet and plant the garden this weekend.

    _____

11. *Him* and *hymn* are homonyms words that have the same sound but different meanings.

    _____

12. Divinity is a soft creamy fudge.

    _____

13. The man driving the car ahead of us keeps checking his map.

    _____

14. The greenhouse effect many scientists agree will alter the earth's climate.

_____

15. The car ran more smoothly after Brian had changed the spark plugs.

_____

16. Hogmanay is New Year's Eve isn't it?

_____

17. Judith carrying two heavy suitcases rushed to make her connecting flight.

_____

18. David is tired hungry and thirsty after working all day in the sun.

_____

19. The Titanic struck an iceberg on April 14 1912 on her maiden voyage.

_____

20. You may write to the author in care of his publisher in Toronto Ontario.

_____

Practice with Semicolons

Basic Rules for Using Semicolons

1. You can use a semicolon alone to join main clauses.

   Trevor drove a stationwagon; his brother drove an MG Midget.

2. You can use a semicolon with a conjunctive adverb (_however, therefore, nevertheless, otherwise, furthermore, then_) to join main clauses.

   There has been a freezing rain; therefore motorists are advised to drive with caution.

3. Use a semicolon with a coordinate conjunction to join main clauses only when the clauses themselves contain internal punctuation.

At times, he could be arrogant, self-serving, and aloof; but he could also be charming, considerate, and courtly.

4. Use semicolons between items in a series when the items have internal punctuation.

For Christmas Darcy wanted only a life-sized, battery-operated robot; a computer with a keyboard, monitor, and hard copy printer; and a colour television with remote control.

Exercise

Add semicolons where necessary to the following sentences.

1. Jake will work for two more years then he plans to retire, buy a small boat, and spend his days fishing.

_____

2. It has been said that art mirrors life it can also be said that life mirrors art.

_____

3. Items at the potluck supper included cold meats such as ham, chicken, and beef Greek salad with tomatoes, onions, and feta cheese and chocolate cake with walnuts, cherries, and butter cream frosting.

_____

4. Simon is very knowledgeable about the subject however, Joseph is better at explaining his ideas to others.

_____

5. I hate having a tooth filled I'm therefore always happy when my dental checkup is good.

_____

6. Ask the travel agent to leave us at least two hours between flights otherwise, we might not clear customs in time to make the connection to Regina.

_____

7. The contractors laid the subflooring then they put up the walls and nailed on the framing for the roof.

_____

8. Several of the stories, especially those dealing with life in a small town, were effective but the judges had hoped for stories dealing with a wider range of subjects.

   _____

9. Some people regard wealth as a means to an end others regard wealth as an end in itself.

   _____

10. Fewer than ten people registered for the course consequently, the section was cancelled.

   _____

Review Exercise 13: Commas and Semicolons

Add commas and semicolons as necessary in the following sentences.

1. Long before the Greeks with their belief in the harmony of the spheres the Chinese considered music to be one of the foundations of government.

   _____

2. Music which represented harmony symbolized the seasons natural phenomena and spiritual essences.

   _____

3. Chinese music the oldest form of Oriental music dates back more than 4500 years however its "golden age" was much more recent occurring during the T'ang dynasty (A.D. 618-907).

   _____

4. Chinese music is based on time Western music in contrast is based on rhythmic and harmonic structure.

   _____

5. Chinese musical instruments were traditionally classified according to the material from which they were constructed: silk (seven-string lute) bamboo (flute) gourd (seventeen-pipe mouth organ) clay (ocarina) metal (bells) stone (chimes) skin (drum) and wood (square trough-like drum).

   _____

6. Western musical instruments however are classified by how they are played not by what they are made of.

_____

7. Unlike Western music Chinese music did not employ a harmonic chord system or counterpoint musicians sang and played in unison.

_____

8. Nevertheless each musician was allowed to add ornamentation that is decorative notes to the melodic line.

_____

9. Early twentieth-century Western composers who were influenced by Chinese music experimented with the twelve-tone scale.

_____

10. Chinese music has also influenced jazz for example jazz pianos are often tuned to flatten the notes and some percussion instruments used in jazz bands originated in China.

_____

Practice with Colons and Dashes

The colon and dash are treated together because there is some overlap in their use. You can use either a colon or a dash to introduce a clause or phrase that explains what comes before it.

He was driven by a single ambition: to be a millionaire before he was thirty.
or
He was driven by a single ambition—to be a millionaire before he was thirty.

A colon is usually a better choice in a formal writing situation, but beware of using too many colons. They can make your writing seem stuffy and stilted. Too many dashes, on the other hand, will make your writing seem choppy and casual.

Basic Rules for Using Colons

1. Use a colon to introduce a list when the list is preceded by a complete clause.

> Police will set up Check Stops at the following locations: the corner of Broadmoor Drive and Lincoln Crescent, the corner of Willow Street and Waters Avenue, and the entrance to the circle road around the university.

2. Do **not** use a colon when the clause that introduces the list is incomplete.

> Police will set up Check Stops at the corner of Broadmoor Drive and Lincoln Crescent, the corner of Willow Street and Waters Avenue, and the entrance to the circle road around the university.

Note: You can use a colon to introduce a list even when the clause that precedes it is incomplete if "as follows" or "the following" is strongly implied.

> Our immediate needs to cope with disaster include:
> 1. canned goods and non-perishable foods
> 2. bedding
> 3. warm clothing for men, women, and children
> 4. tents and sleeping bags

3. Use a colon to introduce an explanatory word or phrase that comes at the end of a sentence.

> She had one main desire when she graduated from high school: never to set foot in a classroom again.

4. Use a colon between main clauses when the second clause explains or emphasizes the first.

> The heat was beyond bearing: people were outside only long enough to move from air-conditioned house to air-conditioned car to air-conditioned office building.

5. Use a colon to introduce a quotation from a book or article if the sentence introducing the quotation is grammatically complete.

> We see the duke's immense arrogance in the following comment: "and I choose / Never to stoop."

Do **not** use a colon when the sentence introducing the quotation is not grammatically complete.

> NOT   The duke says that he: "gave commands; / Then all smiles stopped together."

BUT   The duke says that he "gave commands; / Then all smiles
       stopped together."

6. Use a colon in the following conventional places:

- in biblical references: Ephesians 2:8
- in time references: 8:10, 4:35
- between a title and subtitle: *The English Novel:*
                                  Form and Function

- after the salutation in a   Dear Professor Harkness:
  formal letter: Dear Madam:
                                  Gentlemen:

Basic Rules for Using Dashes

1. You can use the dash to indicate a sudden change in thought or to emphasize a parenthetical remark or an explanatory word or phrase.

   I knew that the mosquito was there—I could hear its insidious whine—and would attack as soon as I fell asleep.
   The dinner—for it was the evening meal—consisted of nothing but a bowl of porridge.

2. Use a dash after a series that introduces a sentence. Use a pair of dashes to set off a series that comes in the middle of a sentence.

   Compassion, courage, and dedication—a nurse must have all these qualities.
   Jeanne has all the qualities—compassion, courage, and dedication—of a good nurse.

Exercise

Add colons and dashes where appropriate.

1. Please bring the following to the next class a dictionary, a handbook of English usage, and the assigned composition text.

   _____

2. Those losing their positions because of the merger the president, two vice-presidents, and the sales manager will receive generous separation allowances.

   _____

3. He was reluctant to admit any knowledge of the matter we had expected he might and refused to say where he had been that night.

_____

4. The dog attacked without provocation the victim said that it did not even bark before leaping at her arm.

_____

5. Shakespeare's sonnet begins as a parody of traditional love sonnets "My mistress' eyes are nothing like the sun."

_____

6. Our next committee meeting is scheduled for Thursday at 8 15 a.m.

_____

7. The company offers the following fringe benefits to all employees a free medical and dental plan, in-house training programs, and professionally staffed day care.

_____

8. The audience sat as though mesmerized they were awed by the magician's brilliant sleight of hand.

_____

9. This picture isn't it beautiful? was painted by my aunt, an artist of considerable talent.

_____

10. After returning from two weeks at summer camp, my brother wanted only two things a double cheeseburger and a large chocolate milkshake.

_____

Practice with Apostrophes

If you are sometimes unsure how and when to use an apostrophe, part of the reason may be that plurals, possessives, and contractions all sound the same. Consider the following examples:

PLURAL	They were lost in the bush for three days. [*days* = plural of *day*]
POSSESSIVE	She lost a day's wages. [*day's* = *of a day*]
CONTRACTION	The day's almost over. [*day's* = *day is*]

An apostrophe indicates **omitted letters** or **possession**. It can also be used to make plural forms of letters (three *A*'s), words referred to as words (four *maybe*'s) and abbreviations (**two Ph.D**'s). It is **not** used to make anything else plural.

Recognizing Plurals, Possessives, and Contractions

You'll have less trouble using the apostrophe correctly if you recognize the differences between plural forms, possessive forms, and contractions.

1. You can make most nouns plural by adding *s* or *es* (*book/books*, *match/matches*). Do **not** use an apostrophe when you want only a plural.

   The **texts** for this course are on reserve in the library.

2. Use an apostrophe when you want to make a noun or an indefinite pronoun possessive.

   Linda's car is in the garage again.
   Somebody's wallet was left on the table.

   Do **not** add an apostrophe to possessive pronouns (*ours, yours, his, hers, its, theirs*).

   The house on the corner is theirs.

3. Use an apostrophe to indicate the omitted letter(s) in a contraction.

   I am = **I'm**
   he would = **he'd**
   someone is = **someone's**

Exercise 1

Indicate whether the italicized word in each of the following sentences is a plural, a possessive, or a contraction.

1. *Everything's* completely backwards in this assignment. _____
2. I missed *today's* traffic report. _____
3. We are eating dinner with the *Greens* tomorrow. _____
4. The boat tied to the dock is *ours*. _____
5. My *sister's* new hair style makes her look like a poodle.
   _____

Using the Apostrophe to Form Certain Plurals

1. Add *'s* to form the plurals of letters and to form the plurals of words referred to as words. Underline the letter or word (to indicate italics), but do not underline the *s*.

> How many **e**'s are there in *beekeeper*?
> When Joan turned on the computer monitor, the screen filled with *hello*'s.

2. Add *'s* to form the plurals of abbreviations.

> **B.A. 's, ICU's, CD's**

3. Add *'s* or *s* alone to form the plurals of numerals and dates.

> During the **1970's** (1970s), the province experienced high unemployment and high inflation.
> Most of my marks in this course have been in the **70's** (70s).

Exercise 2

Make the underlined words plural.

1. in the <u>1930</u> _____
2. five <u>Linda</u> in my grade four class _____
3. ten <u>SPCA</u> in this province _____
4. six <u>*therefore*</u> in this paragraph _____
5. three long <u>*a*</u> in this line of poetry _____

Using the Apostrophe to Form Possessives

1. Add *'s* to form the possessive of indefinite pronouns and singular and plural nouns that do not end with *s*.

> I have picked up **someone's** gloves by mistake.
> Mrs. **Stein's** Himalayan won first prize at the cat show.
> The store has received a new shipment of **children's** clothes.

2. Add *'s* to singular nouns of one syllable ending in *s*.

> The office staff bought a card for Mr. Legree on **Boss's** Day.

3. Add an apostrophe alone to singular nouns of more than one syllable ending in *s*.

> I cannot seem to attract the **waitress'** attention.

4. Add an apostrophe alone to plural nouns ending in *s*.

> He never reads the **critics'** reviews of his plays.

5. Add 's to the last word of compound nouns.

> Robert dented the fender of his brother-in-**law's** new car.

6. Add 's to the last name to show that two or more people own one thing (joint possession).

> **Lisa and Marnie's** room is on the third floor of the residence.

7. Add an apostrophe to all of the names to show that two or more people own things separately (separate possession).

> **Joyce's** and **Beth's** purses were stolen yesterday afternoon.

Note: Possessive nouns do not always refer to people; possessive nouns can also refer to animals and objects.

> The **dog's** paws were wet and muddy.
> The captain assured the port authorities that the **ship's** papers were in order.

Exercise 3

Make the following italicized words possessive.

1. the *stewardesses* _____ wages
2. the *Jacksons* _____ new car
3. *Mark and Lenore* (joint possession)
   _____ bank account
4. *cattle* _____ hooves
5. this pair of *scissors* _____ blades
6. *Tina* and *George* (separate possession) _____ cars
7. the *bee* _____ knees.
8. *Charles* _____ trumpet
9. *sister-in-law* _____ apartment
10. *friendship* _____ reward

Using an Apostrophe to Form Contractions

1. Do not use an apostrophe with a verb unless you are indicating omitted letters.

> NOT   Bill constantly **need's** to borrow money.
> BUT   Bill constantly **needs** to borrow money.

2. Do not confuse the possessive *its* with the contraction *it's* (it is). Never use the form *its'*.

It's unfortunate that you were unable to attend the meeting. [contraction]

The cat licked **its** lips in anticipation. [possessive]

3. Do not confuse the possessive *whose* with the contraction *who's* (who is).

Whose turn is it to do the dishes? [possessive]

Who's sitting beside you at the concert? [contraction]

4. Use an apostrophe to indicate obviously missing numbers in a date.

I last went to San Francisco in the summer of **'69**.

In formal writing, write the date out in full. If the apostrophe is already there to indicate a plural, it's better to leave out the apostrophe indicating an omission.

San Francisco was an exciting place to visit in the late **60's**.

Exercise 4

Add apostrophes where necessary to indicate missing letters and contractions.

1. The dog buried its bone in the garden.

_____

2. Whose car is parked in front of my driveway?

_____

3. Its the opportunity of a lifetime!

_____

4. I went to China in the summer of 86.

_____

5. In the late 80s consumer waste became a major urban concern.

_____

6. Whos the dinner speaker tonight?

_____

7. Id like to come, but Ill have to see if I can get a babysitter.

_____

8. Bill desperately wants his parents to lend him their car.

_____

9. Its near the end of the novel, where the plot becomes completely unbelievable.

_____

10. Shed like to know whos responsible for the mess.

_____

Exercise 5

Add all necessary apostrophes to the following sentences.

1. During the lecture, Tim was absorbed in inscribing a series of linked *I*s around the margins of the page.

_____

2. Flames from the burning garden shed threatened the Martins house.

_____

3. "Weve had a delightful evening," Mrs. Beaulac announced to her hostess, "but Im afraid its time we were leaving."

_____

4. Brendas mother-in-laws afghans were very popular at this years craft sale.

_____

5. The program contains the players scoring statistics for the last two seasons.

_____

6. The issue of free trade between Canada and the United States dominated Canadian politics in the late 1980s.

_____

7. Jim is staying at his parents home while theyre vacationing in British Columbia.

_____

8. Someones keys were found in the washroom, but nobody knows whose.

---

9. There were six *hopefullys*, all of them used incorrectly, in his speech.

---

10. The mens shoe department is on the first floor, right next to childrens wear.

Practice with Italics and Quotation Marks

Basic Rules for Using Italics

1. Italics are indicated by underlining.
2. Underline the titles of books, newspapers, magazines, pamphlets, long poems (that have been published separately), films, plays, television and radio series (*Masterpiece Theatre, This Country in the Morning*), albums and long musical compositions, and works of art.
3. Underline the names of airplanes, ships, trains, and spacecraft. Do not underline abbreviations that come before the name.

   H.M.C.S. *Tecumseh*

4. Underline foreign words and phrases that have not yet been accepted as English terms (*ad infinitum, entre nous*).
5. Underline words referred to as words and letters referred to as letters.

   How many *l*'s are there in *parallel*?

6. Underline words to achieve emphasis.

   Children under six are *not* allowed on the big slide.

Note: Use this technique sparingly.

Exercise 1

Underline where necessary to indicate italics.

1. What is the burglar's modus operandi?
2. Jean-Luc Picard and the crew of the Enterprise carry out their continuing mission on Star Trek: The Next Generation.
3. Our community theatre group is staging a production of Henrik Ibsen's An Enemy of the People.
4. I suggest that you take everything he says cum grano salis.
5. We took the Queen of Saanich ferry to Tsawassen.

Basic Rules for Using Quotation Marks

1. Put quotation marks around titles of most poems, short stories, chapters, articles, songs, individual episodes of television and radio programs.
2. Use quotation marks to set off direct speech. Note that commas and periods go inside the quotation marks.

> Alvin looked directly at Jerry and said, "That's not how I heard the story."

Question marks and exclamation marks also go inside quotation marks if the quotation itself is a question or an exclamation.

> "How are you?" Connie asked. "I haven't seen you in ages."
> "Don't go in there!" he shouted. "The building could collapse at any minute!"

3. Use quotation marks to show that you are incorporating three or more words from another source into your own writing.

PROSE In *Typhoon*, Conrad presents Captain MacWhirr as an ordinary man with "just enough imagination to carry him through each successive day."

POETRY Wordsworth's poem begins with the simile "I wandered lonely as a cloud."

4. Set off long quotations of prose or poetry by triple-spacing before and after the quotation. Indent ten spaces from both margins and single-space the quotation. Do not use quotation marks unless you are quoting dialogue.
5. You can put quotation marks around words referred to as words instead of underlining them.

> "Their" and "there" are frequently confused.

6. Put quotation marks around words used ironically, but do this as little as possible.

I will not engage in a battle of wits with someone who is short of "ammunition."

7. Put quotation marks around translations of terms.

Satis verborum is Latin for "enough of words."

Exercise 2

Punctuate the following sentences correctly.

1. "Where am I" asked Cynthia "Is this a hospital"

_____

2. I'm afraid I planted too much zucchini this year remarked my neighbour, handing me a dozen gigantic squash.

_____

3. Do you think Mrs. Macomber deliberately shot her husband in Hemingway's story The Short Happy Life of Francis Macomber

_____

4. Chez moi means at my house.

_____

5. Who wrote the poem that begins Shall I compare thee to a summer's day

_____

Exercise 3

Use quotation marks and italics correctly in the following sentences.

1. James Thurber's story The Secret Life of Walter Mitty first appeared in The New Yorker in 1939.

_____

2. I can never, asserted Lady Ashley, forgive such barbarous cruelty.

_____

3. The Greek expression eureka means I have found it!

4. The theme of carpe diem (seize the day) reaches its most vivid expression in Andrew Marvell's poem To His Coy Mistress in the lines The grave's a fine and private place / But none, I think, do there embrace.

_____

5. Is the U2 song Angel of Harlem on The Joshua Tree or Rattle and Hum?

_____

6. In the chapter titled The Early Life of the Morels, D. H. Lawrence sets out the reasons for the conflict between Mr. and Mrs. Morel, a conflict that pervades the whole of his early novel, Sons and Lovers.

_____

7. Her favourite Beatles' song is Yesterday.

_____

8. He claims to be an enlightened despot. He is half right, at least.

_____

9. Do you understand my point? Mitch asked, jabbing his pencil into my arm.

_____

10. The motto of the French Revolution was Liberté, Egalité, Fraternité, (Liberty, Equality, Brotherhood).

_____

Practice with Parentheses and Brackets

Basic Rules for Using Parentheses

Use parentheses in the following ways:
1. To set off additional material that interrupts the flow of the sentence.

The shopping expedition (which I thought completely unnecessary) took hours.

2. To enclose explanatory material, such as brief definitions and pieces of historical information.

> You can pick up a calendar (a catalogue briefly describing all college courses) at the main desk when you register.

3. To enclose letters or numerals used to identify items in a list.

> When you are choosing an apartment, be sure to consider (1) rent and the terms of the lease, (2) location, (3) size, (4) parking and laundry facilities.

Do **not** use parentheses:
1. To set off important information.

> I didn't get the money I expected when I traded my car in. (The body was rusted and the brakes needed repair.)

2. Too often. Overuse of parentheses will make your writing choppy and difficult to follow.

> I would have come with you (but I was too busy) to the movie (which I'd already seen).

Punctuation with Parentheses

1. If the material within the parentheses is a complete sentence within another sentence, the parenthetical sentence does not begin with a capital or end with a period.

> My mother (she should know better) promised to lend my brother $100.

2. If the sentence enclosed in parentheses is not part of another sentence, capitalize the first word and put the end punctuation inside the closing parentheses.

> I waited over an hour for him to phone. (I was getting grouchier by the minute!)

Basic Rules for Using Brackets

Use brackets in the following ways:
1. Whenever you insert explanatory material in a quotation. These brackets tell your reader that this material was not part of the original quotation.

> In the first book of *Paradise Lost*, Milton says that Satan, "Stirred up with envy and revenge, deceived / The mother of mankind [Eve]."

2. With the word *sic* (Latin for "thus") to indicate that an error is part of the original quotation.

> The newsletter said that "the principle [*sic*] would be available for consultation on the first day of school."

Exercise

Add parentheses or brackets where appropriate in each of the following sentences.

1. We waited impatiently I must confess for him to appear.
2. The final instructions on the handout stated, "Prooffread *sic* your work carefully."
3. The planes flew in left echelon each plane to the left of the plane in front of it.
4. The Geiger counter is named after the German physicist Hans Geiger 1882-1945.
5. In implementing the plan, we must consider a the cost, b the personnel, and c the amount of time required for completion.

Practice with End Punctuation

Basic Rules for Using Exclamation Marks

1. Most of the time, avoid using exclamation marks in essays and business writing. Don't use exclamation marks often in personal writing, either. Use word choice and sentence structure to create emphasis.
2. Use exclamation marks occasionally

   - after emphatic interjections (No!, Great!)
   - after forceful commands (Come here!)
   - after strong expressions of surprise, anger, disbelief (I'm furious!)

3. When a quotation is an exclamation, put the exclamation mark inside the quotation marks.

> After sitting through the performance, she said "I was never so bored in my life!"

Basic Rules for Using Periods

1. Use a period at the end of

  - a statement (Susan registered for classes today.)
  - an indirect question (She wondered whether she had chosen the right courses.)
  - mild requests and polite commands (Please let me know when you'll be ready to leave.)

2. Use a period with most abbreviations. (M.Ed., Jan., Cres., Rd.)
   Omit the period with abbreviations that are capitalized initials (PCB VCR) or pronounced as words (CUSO, UNICEF). See Abbreviations for more information.

Basic Rules for Using Question Marks

Use a question mark after
1. a direct question (Who's been sleeping in my bed?)
2. tag questions at the end of a sentence (That was a good movie, wasn't it?)
3. each question in a series of short questions (Have you finished washing the dishes? sweeping the floor? taking out the garbage?)
4. a statement intended to express a question (You're finished already?)

Punctuation with Question Marks

1. If the question interrupts a statement, put a question mark after the question.

   My elderly aunt phoned her son in Santiago—do you know where that is?—three times last week.

2. If a quotation is a question, put the question mark inside the quotation marks.

   And then the game show host further excited the audience by asking, "Who wants to win $5000?"

3. If the whole sentence, including the quotation, is a question, put the question mark outside the quotation marks.

   What do you think Hamlet meant when he said, "I am but mad north-north-west; when the wind is southerly I know a hawk from a handsaw"?

Exercise 1

Add exclamation marks, periods, and question marks where appropriate. Put C beside a correct sentence.

1. Giles often wondered whether he could have made it as a professional hockey player

2. Do we have enough raspberries to make pies jam jelly

3. Run for your lives

4. When did Edgar Allan Poe write "The Masque of the Red Death"

5. Although the suspect had a degree in criminology, the RCMP did not hesitate to interrogate him.

Exercise 2

Add exclamation marks, periods, and question marks where appropriate.

1. Astronomers recently discovered the most distant galaxy known to science

2. What is the speed of light

3. Stop doing that immediately

4. The tourists asked the gas station attendant where they could find an inexpensive restaurant

5. I can't do everything at once, can I

6. The first thing he asked was, "What's for dinner"

_____

7. Help Someone is stealing my car

_____

8. Do you agree with the NDP's stand on Canada's participation in NATO

_____

9. My father—did you know he's nearly ninety—travelled across Canada last year on a Greyhound bus

_____

10. What does it mean to say that someone is in "fine fettle"

_____

Review Exercise 14: General Review of Punctuation

Add commas, semicolons, colons, apostrophes, quotation marks, and underlining (to indicate italics) as necessary in the following sentences. Most sentences need several types of punctuation.

1. Murder mysteries are my favourite form of escapist entertainment they provide a brush with danger and a puzzle to solve.

_____

2. Whether on the page or on the screen classic mysteries like Agatha Christies Death on the Nile and the television series Murder She Wrote create a sense of threat that remains securely under control.

_____

3. Although sympathetic characters may be in danger may even hear the ominous words Youre under arrest I know that theyre unlikely to be either victims or murderers.

_____

4. In the worlds created by most mystery writers justice prevails the innocent are spared and the guilty are punished.

_____

5. Its true that as a consequence characterization may be weak.

_____

6. Christies characters are often blatantly stereotypical one exception for reasons I cant mention without giving away the plot is The Murder of Roger Ackroyd.

_____

7. Playgoers and moviegoers must not object to the British writers characters for her play The Mousetrap ran continuously in London for more than thirty years and novels such as Death on the Nile and Murder on the Orient Express have been made into successful films.

_____

8. Too often however Christie depends on descriptive tags such as Hercule Poirots little grey cells to use E. M. Forsters terms from Aspects of Fiction her characters are not round but flat.

_____

9. The characters on Murder She Wrote are sometimes worse the Italian mobsters power-hungry Texas lawyers and ruthless Wall Street financiers on this show are caricatures not merely stereotypes.

_____

10. There is one advantage however to this treatment of character it helps to keep the danger safely at a distance.

_____

11. Danger but not too much danger thats the first requirement of a good mystery.

_____

12. The second requirement is a puzzle which should be neither too easy to solve nor too difficult.

_____

13. When the murderer is revealed I want to exclaim Ah-ha just as I expected but until that moment I want to feel a touch of doubt.

_____

14. The mystery owes this element of the form like so many others to Edgar Allan Poe.

_____

15. Poes short stories The Murders in the Rue Morgue and The Mystery of Marie Roget which Poe called tales of ratiocination present puzzling incongruities that can be resolved only by the astute logical reasoning of Poes amateur detective Auguste Dupin.

_____

16. Dupin is thus a forerunner of that more famous character to whom everything is Elementary my dear Watson Sir Arthur Conan Doyles Sherlock Holmes.

_____

17. The puzzle lies in the identity (and sometimes the motive) of the murderer(s) in traditional mysteries such as those of Dorothy Sayers Michael Innes and Ngaio Marsh all British writers and Dashiell Hammett Raymond Chandler and Ross MacDonald of the American hard-boiled school.

_____

18. Some contemporary mystery writers however depart from this convention for them exploring the psychology of crime is more important than revealing whodunit.

_____

19. Some of Ruth Rendells books especially Judgment in Stone and those published under the pseudonym Barbara Vine examine the impulses that can lead seemingly normal people to commit murder.

_____

20. These books thus bring together what are for me the two delights of murder mysteries the danger and the puzzle come together in Rendells exploration of the darker impulses that lie within us all.

_____

Practice with Abbreviations

Use abbreviations sparingly in general writing. If you intend to use an abbreviation that you think your reader may not understand, write the term out in full the first time you use it, followed by the abbreviation in parentheses. Thereafter, use the abbreviation.

> Over the past few years, the **Canadian Union of Public Employees** (CUPE) has been actively campaigning to improve the job security of its members. CUPE has made several significant gains in this area.

Basic Rules

Names and Titles of People

1. The abbreviated titles *Mr., Mrs., Ms., Dr.* may be used before a person's name (full name, initials and surname, or surname alone).

   > Dr. Samuel Johnson
   > Dr. S. Johnson
   > Dr. Johnson

   The title *St.* may be used before a given name.

   > St. Martin

2. Titles such as Doctor, Saint, Professor, Reverend, Senator, Lieutenant may be abbreviated if the person's first name or initials are given.

   > **Professor Meyers** teaches graduate courses in geophysics.
   > **Prof. Alice Meyers** is a renowned scholar.
   > **Prof. A. S. Meyers** is attending an international conference.

3. Spell out all titles when they are not followed by proper names.

   > He hopes to become a full **professor** by the end of the decade.
   > The **doctor** attended the injured at the scene of the accident.

4. The abbreviations *Jr.* and *Sr.* come after proper names, as do abbreviations of academic degrees. Do not use titles before and after a name if both titles have the same meaning.

   > NOT   Dr. Tyrone Bennett, M.D.
   > BUT   Dr. Tyrone Bennett **or** Tyrone Bennett, M.D.

Names of Organizations, Companies, Agencies

Abbreviations for agencies and organizations usually do not have periods.

NHL	(National Hockey League)
NATO	(North Atlantic Treaty Organization)
UNESCO	(United Nations Educational, Scientific, and Cultural Organization)

Names of Places

Abbreviate the names of provinces, territories, states, and countries and words such as *street, avenue, boulevard, crescent,* and *road* when they are part of the address of an envelope. In most other situations, write out these names in full, except for Union of Soviet Socialist Republics, which is properly expressed as **USSR**.

Dates and Times

1. Use **a.m.** and **p.m.** to refer to **exact** times of the day (9:15 a.m.)
2. The abbreviation B.C. (before Christ) refers to dates before the birth of Christ. A.D. (*anno Domini,* "in the year of our Lord") refers to dates after the birth of Christ. Put B.C. **after** the date and A.D. **before** the date. Do **not** use A.D. when it is obvious that the event occurred after the birth of Christ (after about A.D. 500).

   Julius Caesar invaded Britain in 55 B.C.
   The Roman legions withdrew from Britain in A.D. 410.

3. The names of days and months may be abbreviated in the heading of personal letters; otherwise, write out the names of days, months, and holidays in full.

Units of Measurement

Units such as litre (**L**), metre (**m**), kilometre (**km**), gram (**g**), and kilogram (**kg**) are usually written out except in technical writing and recipes. **Do not use periods with metric abbreviations.**

Scientific and Technical Abbreviations

Some commonly known scientific and technical terms are abbreviated rather than written out.

   TNT (trinitrotoluene), DNA (deoxyribonucleic acid), PCB (polychlorinated biphenyl)

Common Latin Terms

1. It's usually better to use the English equivalents of *e.g.* (*exempli gratia*, "for example") and *i.e.* (*id est*, "that is").
2. Do **not** use *etc.* (*et cetera*) at the end of a list of examples; instead, use the phrase *such as* or *and so forth*. **Never** say *and etc.*

NOT	The pet store sells canaries, macaws, mynahs, etc.
BUT	The pet store sells such birds as canaries, macaws, and mynahs.

The Ampersand (&)

Use this abbreviation only when you are copying a name (Harper & Row, A&W). Do **not** use the ampersand as a substitute for *and* in general writing.

Exercise

Correct all errors in the use of abbreviations. Substitute abbreviations for long forms where appropriate.

1. Sherlock Holmes relied on his able assist., Doctor Watson.

_____

2. Rev. O'Connor led the Remembrance Day service.

_____

3. This year we plan to spend Xmas skiing at Jasper, AB.

_____

4. Pontius Pilate, Procurator of Judea, anno Domini 26-36, is remembered for his role in the condemnation and execution of Jesus.

_____

5. Prof. Whiteley will arrive at the airport at 6:30 post meridiem.

_____

6. Mrs. C.D. Laing, Junior, has agreed to organize the auction.

_____

7. Dr. James Lee, M.D., has retired after a long and distinguished career as a heart specialist.

_____

8. Socrates (469-399 before Christ) was a constant irritant to the Athenian authorities.

_____

9. Summer courses run from the beginning of July to the first week in Aug.

_____

10. It's approximately five km between home and the office.

_____

11. Roger McKerracher, Doctor of Philosophy, is a prof. in the hist. dept.

_____

12. Eileen & Carol are majoring in phys. ed.

_____

13. The folk festival in Winnipeg, MB, drew fans from all over Canada.

_____

14. The water main on River Rd. burst, causing flood damage to several homes.

_____

15. She will be working for eight months in Paris with the United Nations Educational, Scientific, and Cultural Organization.

_____

16. Mister & Mrs. Chimko celebrated their thirtieth wedding ann.

_____

17. New York is one of the most interesting cities to visit in the U.S.

_____

18. *Laser, maser, radar,* etc. are acronyms that are now considered common nouns.

_____

19. The baby, born Sept. 28, weighed 3.6 kg.

_____

20. Trinitrotoluene is a high explosive used e.g. in artillery shells.

_____

Practice with Capitalization

Basic Rules

1. Capitalize the first word of every sentence.
2. Capitalize the first word of a direct quotation if the quotation is a complete sentence.

> "May I have your autograph?" the fan asked. "It's for my young niece."

Note: Do **not** capitalize the first word of a quotation that is not a complete sentence.

> The store clerks were instructed to tell all their customers to "have a nice day."

3. Capitalize proper nouns. They name particular people, places, and things and include the following:

- **Names of specific people**

> Alice Munro, John A. Macdonald, Dorothy, Aunt Elizabeth, Uncle John, Captain Brown, Professor Watson

Note: Terms for family relationships and formal titles are capitalized only when they are part of a proper noun or when they act as a substitute for a proper name without a possessive pronoun.

> Ask Cousin Wilbur whether he wants another piece of pie.
> My cousin has a voracious appetite.

> Last year Mother and Father celebrated their fortieth wedding anniversary.
> Last year my mother and father celebrated their fortieth wedding anniversary.

- **Names of specific places, including geographical names and the names of specific streets, avenues and highways**

Note: Names of directions are **not** capitalized unless they are part of proper names or act as place names.

> We were exhausted after a shopping expedition to the West Edmonton Mall.
> To many Western Canadians, "down East" means anywhere east of Winnipeg.

- **Names of planets, stars and other heavenly bodies**

Note: Do **not** capitalize *sun* and *moon*, and do **not** capitalize *Earth* when it is modified by the definite article *the*.

> Mercury, Venus, and Earth are the first three planets revolving around our sun.
> Much of the earth is covered with water.

- **Names of institutions, political parties, organizations, and branches of government**

> the University of Toronto
> the Liberal Party, a Conservative politician
> Alcoholics Anonymous
> Department of Vital Statistics

- **Nationalities, languages, religious groups, sacred and religious names**

> Canadian, Australian, German
> English, French, Swahili
> Christian, Jewish, Buddhist
> God, the Saviour, Allah, Shiva
> New Testament, the Pentateuch, the Koran

- **Days of the week, the months, holidays, events**

> Friday, Saturday
> November, December
> Remembrance Day, Halloween
> the Renaissance, World War II

Note: The names of the seasons—summer, winter, spring, fall—are **not** capitalized.

- **Names of specific school courses**

> Philosophy 200, Physics 301

Note: The names of general subjects, except languages, are **not** capitalized.

This year Evelyn has registered for courses in psychology, statistics, chemistry, and Latin.

4. Capitalize the first, last, and all important words in titles of books, newspapers, magazines, plays, short stories, articles, musical compositions, and movies.

Note: Do **not** capitalize *the*, *a*, or *an* or short conjunctions and prepositions unless they are the first word of the title.

Lives of Girls and Women
A Jest of God
The Creature from the Black Lagoon

Exercise

Correct all errors in capitalization by adding necessary capitals and deleting unnecessary ones.

1. Perhaps the most famous mutiny in History occurred in 1789 on HMS *bounty* when Fletcher Christian and a group of mutineers seized the ship from captain William Bligh and set him and his followers adrift in the south Pacific.

_____

2. Michel, mother wants you to write a letter to aunt Rose thanking her for the socks she sent for christmas.

_____

3. The High School drama students are staging a victorian melodrama this year.

_____

4. On our tour of Ontario, we visited brock's monument at queenston heights.

_____

5. Yvan studied french at the Sorbonne for a year.

_____

6. Yesterday my brother asked me, "do you believe that there is intelligent life in the universe?"

   _____

7. "It's possible, "I replied, "That we have already received communication from some form of extraterrestrial intelligence."

   _____

8. The Northernmost constellation is Ursa Minor, also known as the Little bear. Its most important star is polaris, the north Star.

   _____

9. In the 1951 film production of Tennessee Williams' *A streetcar named desire*, marlon brando recreated his stage role of Stanley Kowalski.

   _____

10. Mitchell refused to listen to his Doctor's advice about the hazards of High Blood Pressure.

    _____

11. Aicha will be taking sociology 200 and english 210 in the Fall term.

    _____

12. Whenever uncle Tobias has to attend a formal dinner party, he says that he feels "Like a fish out of water."

    _____

13. During world war II, when did the invasion of europe by Allied Forces begin?

    _____

14. In rush hour traffic it can take an hour to drive from the North to the South side of the city.

    _____

15. Anthony, who had not studied for the Latin exam, translated *sic transit gloria mundi* as "Gloria was ill in the subway on Monday."

    _____

Practice with Hyphens

Basic Rules for Hyphenating Words at the End of Lines

Avoid hyphenating words at the end of lines whenever you can. When you do need to hyphenate because you can't squeeze all the letters on one line, follow these guidelines:

1. Do **not** hyphenate one-syllable words.
2. Do **not** hyphenate words of six or fewer letters.
3. Do **not** hyphenate figures ($15.95), dates, and abbreviations.
4. Do **not** hyphenate the last word of more than two consecutive lines, the last word in a paragraph, or the last word on a page.
5. Hyphenate between syllables. The first part of the word must contain at least three letters. Try to divide the word into two approximately equal parts that convey the sense of the word.

Exercise 1

Some of these words are correctly hyphenated and some are not. If the word is correctly hyphenated, put C beside it. If the word is incorrectly hyphenated, correct the error.

1. ca-lendar _____
2. dietar-y _____
3 fil-ling _____
4. her-oism _____
5. drop-ped _____
6. UNICEF _____
7. aban-don _____
8. wrap-ping _____
9. nev-ertheless _____
10. medi-um _____

Conventional Uses of the Hyphen

1. Hyphens are used to form some compound words.

mother-in-law	touch-and-go
great-grandfather	green-eyed
galley-slave	leg-of-mutton sleeve

Other compound words are written as separate words (party politics) or as one word (stepsister, manhandle). For current usage consult a good, up-to-date dictionary. If different dictionaries give different forms of the same word, choose one form and use it consistently.

2. Use a hyphen to form **two-word numbers** from twenty-one to ninety-nine and with **fractions** used as adjectives or adverbs.

> Thirty-five students have registered for the course.
> He owns a one-half interest in the company.

Note: Do **not** hyphenate fractions used as nouns.

> I have completed about two thirds of the book.

3. Hyphenate **compound modifiers** (two or more words acting as a single adjective and conveying a single concept) that come **before** a noun.

> well-deserved vacation
> apple-green carpet
> twentieth-century technology

Note: If a compound modifier contains an *ly* adverb, do **not** hyphenate it.

> prominently displayed notice
> carefully concealed passageway
> hastily constructed shack

4. The prefixes *self* (self-congratulatory), *ex* (ex-wife), and *all* (all-terrain), and the suffix *elect* (president-elect) take hyphens.

Note: Do **not** use a hyphen with *self* when it is the root (selfhood, selfish).

5. Hyphenate prefixes that come before nouns beginning with a capital.

> anti-Jacobean
> post-World War II
> pro-British

6. Use a hyphen to avoid an awkward combination of letters or to prevent misreading.

> pre-election
> semi-independent
> re-mark (mark again)
> two-day-old puppies
> two day-old puppies

7. Use hyphens to show that two or more prefixes are attached to a single root.

> Both pro- and anti-union speakers shared the stage.
> The company is hiring both full- and part-time workers.

Exercise 2

Using a dictionary for reference, write each of the following correctly as one word, separate words, or a hyphenated word.

1. father in law
2. self indulgent
3. anti American
4. lily of the valley
5. lily livered
6. ex stock broker
7. quickly scribbled note
8. two thirds empty
9. mouth wash
10. ground zero
11. landed immigrant
12. great aunt
13. eighty seven
14. eel like aquatic vertebrate
15. fusion bomb
16. well written paper
17. mayor elect
18. keep sake
19. out fielder
20. black board

Exercise 3

Add hyphens where necessary.

1. Tanya has a part time job as a sales clerk in an electronics store.
2. People are generally turned off by his holier than thou attitude.
3. The party leaders are engaging in some preelection campaigning.
4. The professors edited an anthology of nineteenth and twentieth century poetry.
5. Beatrice, who is left handed, can't use ordinary scissors.
6. The band played honky tonk music in a cheap cabaret.
7. He's a bit too devil may care for my taste.
8. Twenty three children in the school have come down with the new strain of flu.
9. How could she be such a small minded, ill tempered, contemptibly selfish person?
10. The sirens sounded the all clear when the air raid was over.

Practice Using Numbers

Basic Rules

1. Use numerals (**79**) rather than words (**seventy-nine**) for numbers in scientific and technical writing.
2. In general writing, use numerals
   - if you are providing a series of numbers
   - to express a number that takes more than two words to spell out (**310**)

- to express exact times of day (**8:45**) and with a.m. and p.m. (**9:00 a.m.**)
- to express dates (**10 December 1978** or **December 10, 1978**)
- to express addresses (**#301 11746 122 Street**)
- to express percentages (**36 percent**) and decimals (**3.9 cm**)
- to express page, verse, act, and scene numbers in literary works

3. In general writing, use words

- for numbers that can be spelled out in one or two words
- to express round numbers with money (**ten** dollars), measurements (**six** metres), times (**ten** o'clock)
- to express centuries (**nineteenth** century)
- when you begin a sentence with a number (**Ten** people were present.)

Note: Use a combination of words and numerals to prevent confusion (He ordered **ten 37 cent** stamps).

Exercise

Correct the use of numbers in the following sentences. Put *C* beside a correct sentence.

1. Sally tries to get to school by 8 o'clock every day.

2. $15 seems like a lot to pay for lunch.

3. Please meet me at 9:15 sharp.

4. Last year 10 000 needy families were helped by the Christmas Bureau.

5. Our enrolment figures are up five percent this year.

6. I need to get fourteen 3 cm X 12 cm pieces of wood for my project.

7. He won $ 10 000 000 in a lottery on September thirtieth, 1989.

8. 1200 angry protesters marched in front of the legislative buildings.

9. Can you lend me ten dollars and ninety-five cents so that I can buy the text for the course?

10. The food bank helped 345 families in February and 458 families in March. By April the number of families relying on the food bank had increased to 602.

_____

Review Exercise 15: General Review of Abbreviations, Capitalization, Hyphens, and Numbers

Correct all errors in the use of abbreviations, capitalization, hyphens, and numbers.

1. Lieutenant Jennifer Wong has invited her Mother to visit her at North Atlantic Treaty Organization military headquarters in brussels, belg.

_____

2. 30 000 troops from the U.S., Canada and western Europe are gathering to celebrate the signing of a new treaty with the warsaw pact countries on May first.

_____

3. Genls. from all the member countries will review the smartly uniformed troops as crowds of 1 000s line the gaily decorated streets.

_____

4. The spectacle will rival those in Biblical movie epics set in the 1st few centuries Anno domini, with their roman legions and blood-thirsty tyrants.

_____

5. The arctic archipelago lies North of Mainland Canada.

_____

6. These islands, with their intervening waters, cover 1.3 million km 2.

_____

7. 6 of the world's 30 largest islands belong to this group, the biggest being baffin I.

_____

8. The Eastern islands in this archipelago are mountainous, some peaks rising over 2000 m.

_____

9. Alexander Graham bell was born at edinburgh, scot., on Mar. 3, 1847, and died at Baddeck, N.S., on the second of august 1922.

_____

10. Known for the founding of the Bell tel co. in the US, Bell also supported the work of other scientists, notably that of Professor A. A. Michelson, who was awarded the nobel prize in physics in 1907.

_____

11. Among 19th and 20th century inventors, Bell is considered second only to Thomas Alva Edison.

_____

12. The Dionne quintuplets attracted world wide attention in the 1930s.

_____

13. The ont. govt., fearing the quintuplets would be exploited, removed them from their Father and Mother and placed them under the care of Dr. Allan Roy Dafoe, M.D., the dr. who had delivered them.

_____

14. Their mother fought a 9 year battle to regain custody, but the reunion in Nov. 1943 was a failure.

_____

15. Meanwhile, the dionne babies became a tourist attraction worth 500 000 000 dollars to the provincial Government; 3 million people came to "Quintland" to watch them play behind a one way screen.

_____

16. At 11 o'clock on Nov. 11, cannons across Canada fire to commemorate the Armistice that ended WWI in 1918.

_____

17. The Royal Can. Legion distributes poppies in honour of those who died in flanders and elsewhere.

_____

18. During the war of 1812, Laura Secord walked 30 km. to warn a british Officer of American plans to attack.

_____

19. The Canadian Broadcasting Company will carry the stanley cup final at six p.m.

_____

20. Lord Stanley, gov. genl. of Canada, donated the much coveted cup in 1893; it was presented to a number of amateur hockey champions before it came under the control of the N. H. L. in 1926.

_____

PART 3

HOW WORDS WORK

If you sometimes think that no one but a teacher cares about spelling errors, consider for a moment whether you would get your hair cut in a place where the sign on the window read "No apointments Neccesary."

Spelling errors in letters, reports, and essays undermine your credibility. At best, they are distracting; at worst, they make you seem less intelligent and competent than you really are. If you are a poor speller, you may limit yourself to the words you know how to spell, a strategy that restricts your vocabulary and the precision with which you can express your ideas. More effective strategies for coping with poor spelling include the following:

1. Proofread very carefully. One technique is to read your paper in reverse order, beginning with the last sentence.
2. Take spelling seriously and make a conscious effort to memorize the correct spellings of words you frequently misspell.
3. Use a dictionary whenever you are in any doubt about the correct spelling of a word.
4. Ask someone whose spelling you trust to proofread for you.
5. Use a spelling checker if you do written assignments on a word processor.
6. Memorize the basic spelling rules listed below. They won't eliminate every spelling error, but they will help.

13
Basic Spelling Rules

For Noun Plurals

Nouns are words that name people, places, and things. The guidelines below cover the basic spelling rules for forming the plurals of nouns.

1. Most nouns form the plural by adding *s* to the singular.

   one house/two houses
   one tree/many trees
   one desk/several desks

2. If the word ends in *s, ss, sh, ch,* or *x,* add *es.*

   one wish/three wish**es**
   an actress/several actress**es**
   one match/a book of match**es**

3. Some nouns that end in *f* or *fe* change the ending to *ve* and add *s.*

   one life/nine li**ves**
   one knife/three kni**ves**
   one leaf/a pile of lea**ves**

   Other nouns that end in *f* add only *s.*

   sheriff/sheriffs
   roof/roofs

4. Nouns ending in *o* add either *s* or *es.* If the *o* is preceded by a vowel, always add only *s*

   patio/patios
   radio/radios

piano/pianos
hero/heroes
potato/potatoes

5. Proper nouns (usually names) ending in *y* form their plurals by adding *s*.

Mary/Marys
Larry/Larrys

6. Common nouns ending in *y* preceded by a consonant form their plurals by changing the *y* to *i* and adding *es*.

country/countries
secretary/secretaries
spy/spies

7. Common nouns ending in *y* preceded by a vowel form their plurals by adding only *s*.

Attorney/attorneys
valley/valleys

8. Compound Nouns
To form the plural of most compound nouns, add *s*.

stage-hand/stage-hands
lieutenant-colonel/lieutenant-colonels

In some compound nouns, the most important word in the compound is made plural.

mother-in-law/mothers-in-law
attorney-general/attorneys-general
commander-in-chief/commanders-in-chief

9. Irregular Plurals
Some words have irregular plurals.

child/children
man/men
woman/women
die/dice

Some words, usually animal names, have the same form for both singular and plural.

deer/deer
sheep/sheep
fish/fish (or fishes)

230

10. Foreign Words

Some of these have retained their foreign plurals.

analysis/ analyses
thesis/ theses
crisis/ crises
datum/ data
medium/ media
criterion/ criteria
phenomenon/ phenomena
stimulus/ stimuli

The plurals of other foreign words are in transition. Their foreign plural forms are still accepted, but they have alternate plural forms that follow the regular English pattern.

memorandum/ memoranda or memorandums
curriculum/ curricula or curriculums
formula/ formulae or formulas

Exercise 1

Write the plural form of each of the following nouns.

1. company _____
2. handkerchief _____
3. woman _____
4. baby _____
5. thief _____
6. cupful _____
7. half _____
8. criterion _____
9. hero _____
10. sister-in-law _____

For Words Containing *ie*/*ei*

Most people are familiar with the old rhyme

Use *i* before *e*
except after *c*
or when sounded as *a*
as in *neighbour* and *weigh*.

This rhyme is a useful device that covers many of the words containing *ie* or *ei*, as the following examples illustrate.

- Use *i* before *e*: believe, piece, convenient, mischief, yield, niece, achieve, patient
- Except after *c*: receive, perceive, conceit, conceivable
- Or when sounded as *a*: sleigh, freight, reign

There are, however, more exceptions to the basic rule than those referred to in the rhyme.

Exceptions

1. Use *ei* when the vowels are pronounced as a long *i*: height, seismograph.
2. Use *ei* when the vowels are pronounced as a short *i* after *f*: counterfeit, forfeit, surfeit.
3. Use *ie* after *c* in words containing the letters *cien* (pronounced *shen*): sufficient, ancient, efficient, proficiency.
4. Use *ei* in these common exceptions: foreign, seize, weird, leisure, heir, their.

For Adding Suffixes

To Words Ending in *e*

1. Drop the final *e* when adding a suffix beginning with a vowel, including *y*.

   dense + ity = density
   write + ing = writing
   craze + y = crazy

   Exceptions: hoe + ing = hoeing; canoe + ing = canoeing

   More Exceptions: Keep the *e* when adding a suffix beginning with *a, o, or u* to words ending in *ce* or *ge*.

   courage + ous = courageous
   advantage + ous = advantageous
   notice + able = noticeable

2. Keep the final *e* when adding a suffix beginning with a consonant.

   nine + ty = ninety
   hope + less = hopeless
   absolute + ly = absolutely

Exceptions: wholly, truly, duly, ninth, awful, argument

3. When adding *ing* to words ending in *ie*, change the *ie* to *y*.

lie + ing = **lying**
die + ing = **dying**
tie + ing = **tying**

To Words Ending in *y*

1. When the word ends in a consonant and *y*, change the *y* to *i* before adding all suffixes except *ing*.

mystery + ous =myster**ious**
satisfactory + ly = satisfactor**ily**
deny + ing = den**ying**

Exceptions: one-syllable words, such as *shy* (*shyness*) and *dry* (*dryness*)

2. When a word ends in a vowel and *y*, keep the *y* when adding any kind of suffix.

employ + ee = emplo**yee**
betray + al = betra**yal**
destroy + ing = destro**ying**

Exceptions: Some one-syllable words, such as *day* (*daily*), *pay* (*paid*), *say* (*said*), *lay* (*laid*), *slay* (*slain*)

To Words Ending in a Consonant

1. Double the final consonant when adding a suffix beginning with a vowel, including *y*, to the following types of words.

   • A one-syllable word that ends in a single vowel followed by a single consonant.

   plan + ing = **planning**
   ship + ed = **shipped**
   wrap + ing = **wrapping**

   • A word of more than one syllable that ends in a single vowel followed by a single consonant. The accent must fall on the last syllable of the word and remain there in the new word.

   regret + able = regre**ttable**
   prefer + ed = prefe**rred**
   confer + ed = confe**rred**

occur + ed = occurred
occur + ence = occurrence

But: preference, conference, benefited. The accent in these words is on the first syllable.

2. Do not double the final consonant when adding a suffix that begins with a consonant.

equip + ment = equipment
allot + ment = allotment
dim + ly = dimly

3. Add a *k* to words ending in *ic* when adding a suffix that begins with a vowel

picnic + ing = picnicking
panic + ed = panicked
mimic + ing = mimicking

Exercise 2

Correct the fifteen spelling errors in the following paragraph.

There can be little arguement that learning to be a good speller is fraught with difficultys. It has even been sayd that there are many more exceptions than rules in English spelling. While this sentiment may be somewhat exaggerated, there are sufficeint exceptions to send even the most adept spellers runing to their dictionarys. Moreover, for some mysteryous reason, English contains numerous words that have very different pronunciations for the same spelling. *Hieght* and *freight*, for example, sound nothing alike; nor do *bough, slough,* and *enough*. It's also true that English includes words that do sound the same but have noticably different spellings, such as *thier, they're,* and *there; brake* and *break;* and *cite, sight,* and *site.* Such homonyms are easly confused. In fact, even computers that have "spell check" features won't recognize an incorrectly spelled homonym. To add to the confusion, Canadian English contains a number of spellings that differ from American spellings. *Honour, valour, centre, metre,* and *theatre* are prefered Canadian spellings. *Honor, valor, center, meter,* and *theater* are American. Given these idiosyncrasies, spelling accurately is at times a trying business, but a good writer has no choice but to maintain a continuous guard against the gremlin-like spelling errors that creep into the workings of even the most carefully revised peice of writting.

14
Using a Dictionary

A good dictionary of current English can give you some very useful information.

Spelling

The basic spelling rules do not cover all the words that are frequently misspelled. You can use a dictionary to look up the spelling. If two spellings are given, the first is the more common. Be sure to note whether the dictionary is Canadian or American. For example, the Canadian spelling for what you get on payday is a *cheque*; the American equivalent is a *check*.

Exercise 1: Spelling

Some of the words in the list are spelled correctly, and some are not. If the word is correctly spelled, write C beside it. If not, write the correct spelling beside it. Use a dictionary to check your work.

1. achievement _____
2. athelete _____
3. occurrance _____
4. inconvient _____
5. priviledge _____
6. definately _____
7. develope _____
8. existence _____
9. tradegy _____
10. fundemental _____

Syllabication

Most dictionaries indicate syllable divisions with a centred dot between each syllable.

> syl • la • ble
> dic • tion • ar • y
> spell • ing

It's easier to pronounce an unfamiliar word when you know the syllable divisions. If you need to hyphenate a word, be sure to divide it between syllables.

Exercise 2: Syllabication

Using a dictionary as a guide, divide each of the following words into syllables.

1. heavenly _____
2. implement _____
3. kindliness _____
4. dinosaur _____
5. modify _____
6. amazement _____
7. altogether _____
8. occurrence _____
9. pinafore _____
10. reunion _____

Pronunciation

Dictionaries vary somewhat in the symbols they use to give the pronunciation of a word. This information is usually given in parentheses after the entry word. The key to these symbols may be located in the introduction to the dictionary or at the bottom of the entry page. The key tells you what sounds the symbols used in phonetic spelling stand for.

One very common symbol is the **schwa** (∂), which is used to represent the unstressed vowel sound in an unstressed syllable. The sound of a schwa is very close to *uh*. A heavy accent mark (′) placed after a particular syllable indicates that this syllable receives the primary stress. A lighter accent mark (′) following a syllable indicates that it receives a weak or secondary stress. Note the phonetic spellings of the following words:

incommunicable   (in´kə myoo´nə kə bəl)
scientific   (sī ən tif´ ik)
hypothesis   (hī poth´ ə sis)
theorize   (thē´ ə rīz

If you are looking up an unfamiliar word, use the pronunciation guide and practice saying the word aloud. It's hard to remember a word you can't pronounce.

Exercise 3

Write the word indicated by each of the following phonetic spellings:

1. ri lī´ _____
2. in´ vən tōr´ ē _____
3. āl´ yən ā´ shən _____
4. mas´ tər fəl _____
5. kon´ she en´ shəs _____
6. or nə men´ təl _____
7. yoo´ nə form _____
8. ri vurs´ _____
9. par´ shə lē _____
10. hos´ pi təl _____

Parts of Speech

A dictionary will tell you whether the word you are looking up is a noun (n.), a pronoun (pron.), a transitive verb (v.t.), an intransitive verb (v.i.), an adjective (adj.), an adverb (adv.), a preposition (prep.), a conjunction (conj.) or an interjection (interj.). More than one part of speech will be given for some words, since the part of speech depends upon the function of the word in the sentence.

This skillet is made of cast **iron** [noun].
I never **iron** [verb].
That child has an **iron** [adjective] will.

A **transitive verb** takes an object.

Mary **ate cereal** for breakfast.

An **intransitive verb** does not take an object and is often followed by a prepositional phrase.

They **looked at** the picture.

Knowing what part of speech a word is will help you to use it correctly in your own speech and writing. If you know that *waive*, for example, is a verb meaning "to refrain from claiming a right," you won't be tempted to use it as if it were a noun.

RIGHT   He **waived** his dower rights as part of the divorce settlement.

WRONG   He signed the **waive** as part of the divorce settlement.

Exercise 4: Parts of Speech

Give the part of speech of each of the following words.

1. facade _____
2. gnaw _____
3. golly _____
4. because _____
5. honestly _____
6. breathless _____
7. advise _____
8. listen _____
9. capable _____
10. capacity _____

Etymology

Etymology is information about the origins of a word. The guide at the beginning of the dictionary will explain the meaning of the symbols used in the entry. The etymology of a word is likely to be included only in fairly large dictionaries, where it may be placed in brackets after the word or after the definition.

wail [ME *weile*; perh. OE *weila* cf. OE *waelan* to torment, Icel *weala* to wail]

This information tells us that our modern English word *wail* probably came from the Icelandic word meaning "wail" and the Old English word meaning "to torment." These forms combined in the Middle English word *weile*, which means the same as our modern English *wail*.

Exercise 5: Etymology

Underline the language from which each English word is originally derived.

1. cookie	a) Spanish	b) Dutch	c) French
2. piano	a) Old Norse	b) German	c) Italian
3. verbose	a) Latin	b) Greek	c) Sanskrit
4. potlatch	a) French	b) Chinook	c) Old English
5. gung ho	a) German	b) Gaelic	c) Chinese

Meanings

Most dictionaries give the most common meaning of the word first. If the word is used as more than one part of speech, the more common use is given first. *Loose,* for instance, can be both an adjective and a verb, but its more usual meaning as an adjective would be given first. As the examples below illustrate, it's often important to look at all the meanings so that you can choose the one that best fits the context in which the word is used.

charm (n.) 1. the ability to delight, enchant, captivate
2. a trinket worn on a necklace, bracelet, etc.
3. an object or action assumed to have occult power

pickle (n.) 1. brine, vinegar, or spicy solution used to preserve vegetables, meat, or fish
2. a vegetable served in that condition
3. a difficult situation; plight

Exercise 6: Meanings

Give two different definitions for each of the following words. After each definition, use the word in a short phrase. Be sure that the context you give is appropriate to the definition.

Example: letter a) a symbol representing a speech sound (the letter *a*)
b) a written or printed message (a letter of application)

1. lie   a) _____

    b) _____

2. cone   a) _____

    b) _____

3. drop   a) _____

    b) _____

4. game a) _____

b) _____

5. foot a) _____

b) _____

Glossary of Grammatical Terms

Active Voice

A construction in which the subject performs the action of the verb,

> Lightning struck the enormous tree

In the passive voice, the sentence would read:

> The enormous tree was struck by lightning.

Adjective

A word that modifies a noun or pronoun. An adjective can express quality (*red* balloon, *large* house, *young* child) or quantity ('*one* apple, *many* peaches, *few* pears). Other words or grammatical constructions can also function as adjectives, including present and past participles (*skating* party, *torn* shirt and subordinate clauses (the woman *who is chairing the meeting*).

Adjectives change form to show degrees of comparison—positive, comparative, superlative (clean, cleaner, cleanest).

Adverb

A word that modifies or describes a verb (run *quickly*), an adjective (*extremely* heavy), or another adverb (eat *very* slowly). Adverbs usually answer the questions *how, when, where* or *why*. (They whispered how? / They whispered quietly.)

Phrases (*walked into a room*) and clauses (He couldn't speak *because he was angry*) can also function as adverbs.

Adverbs change form to show degrees of comparison—positive, comparative, superlative (quickly, more quickly, most quickly).

Antecedent

The noun to which the pronoun refers. The antecedent usually comes before the pronoun.

> The **dancers** [antecedent] are rehearsing **their** [pronoun] routine.

Appositive

An explanatory word or phrase that follows a noun.

> Martha, **my closest friend**, is visiting from Halifax.

Auxiliary Verb

A verb that helps to form the tense or voice of another verb (*have been* practicing, *should have* phoned, *was* consulted).

Case

The form of a noun or pronoun that shows its relationship to other words in a sentence.

> Possessive case (nouns and indefinite pronouns): **Bill's** car, **nobody's** business.
> Subject case (personal pronouns): **She** and **I** left early.
> Object case (personal pronouns): Give the message to **me** or **him**.

Clause

A group of words containing a subject and a verb. **Main clauses** can stand on their own as grammatically complete sentences.

> He didn't finish dinner.

Some **subordinate clauses**, sometimes called dependent clauses, begin with subordinate conjunctions such as *because, although, while, since, as, when.*

> **Because he was in a hurry,** he didn't finish dinner.

Other subordinate clauses begin with relative pronouns such as *who, which,* and *that.* These subordinate clauses function as adjectives or nouns.

> The man **who didn't finish dinner** is in a bad mood. [adjective clause]
> She wished **that the ordeal would end.** [noun clause]

Comma Fault (also called *Comma Splice*)

A sentence structure error in which main clauses have been joined by a comma alone.

The party is over, everyone has gone home.

The main clauses may also have been joined by a comma and a conjunctive adverb.

The party is over, **therefore** everyone must go home.

Complex Sentence

A sentence containing one main clause and one or more subordinate clauses. See *Clause*.

If we can't fit everyone in the car, we'll take the bus.

Compound-Complex Sentence

A sentence containing two or more main clauses and one or more subordinate clauses.

Before the storm broke, Mary put away the lawn chairs and Shistri closed the windows.

Compound Sentence

A sentence containing two or more main clauses. See *Clause*.

We can't fit everyone in the car, so we'll take the bus.

Conjunction

A word or phrase that joins words, phrases, or clauses. See *Conjunctive Adverb, Coordinate Conjunction, Correlative (Paired) Conjunctions,* and *Subordinate Conjunction*.

Conjunctive Adverb

An adverb used with a semicolon to join main clauses in a compound or compound-complex sentence. Common conjunctive adverbs include *therefore, however, nevertheless, otherwise, thus, furthermore, moreover*.

I must hurry; **otherwise,** I'll be late for class.

Coordinate Conjunction

A word used to join ideas of equal importance expressed in the same grammatical form. The coordinate conjunctions are *and, but, or, nor, for, yet, so*.

He was down **but** not out.
The weather was good, **but** the facilities were terrible.

Coordination

The stylistic technique of using coordinate and correlative conjunctions to join ideas of equal importance. See *Coordinate Conjunction* and *Correlative (Paired) Conjunctions*.

> The battery is dead **and** all four tires are flat.
> **Neither** the fridge **nor** the stove is working.

Correlative (Paired) Conjunctions

A pair of conjunctions used to join ideas of equal importance expressed in the same grammatical form. The correlative conjunctions are *either/or, neither/nor, both/and, not only/but also*.

> **Not only** are these apples expensive **but** they are **also** of poor quality.
> These apples are **both** expensive **and** of poor quality.

Dangling Modifier

A modifying phrase that is not logically connected to any other word in the sentence.

> **Turning green,** the pedestrians crossed the street.

Definite Article

The word *the,* which specifies the noun it is describing: *the* book, *the* baby, *the* opportunity of a lifetime.

Fragment

A phrase or subordinate clause punctuated as if it were a complete sentence.

> And last, but not least.
> Although it seemed like a good idea at the time.

Fused Sentence (also called *Run-on Sentence*)

The error of writing two main clauses as if they were one with no punctuation between them.

> It's cold today my ears are freezing.

Indefinite Article

The words *a* and *an,* which do not specify the nouns they describe: *a* book, *a* breakthrough, *an* amazing feat.

Infinitive

To + a verb: to run, to walk, to think. See *Split Infinitive*.

Interjection

A word or phrase thrown into a sentence to express emotion.

> "**Oh great**, we're going on a picnic!"
> "**For Pete's sake**, I knew that already."

Some interjections can stand on their own as complete sentences.

> "Wow!" "Ouch!" "Hurray!"

Misplaced Modifier

A modifying word, phrase, or clause that has been put in the wrong place in the sentence.

> **Lying in the driveway**, Mr. Jones drove over the bicycle.

Mixed Construction (sometimes called an *Awkward Sentence*)

The error of mixing incompatible grammatical units.

> **An example of this is when** she daydreams constantly. [putting a subordinate clause after a linking verb]
> The more he learns, he doesn't seem to remember much. [failing to complete a pattern]

Modifier

A word, phrase, or clause that changes or qualifies the meaning of a noun, pronoun, or verb.

Restrictive modifiers provide essential information and are not enclosed in commas.

> Teenagers **who take drugs** need help.

Nonrestrictive modifiers provide additional information and are enclosed with commas.

> Susan, **who has been taking drugs for several years**, needs help.

Mood

The form of the verb that shows whether the speaker is stating a fact (indicative mood: He *wants* some food), giving a command or making a request (imperative mood: *Give him* some food), or suggesting a possibility or condition (subjunctive mood: *If we were to give* him some food).

Noun

A word that names a person, place, thing, quality, idea, or activity. A **common noun** is not capitalized and refers to any one of a class: *woman, cat, city, school*. A **proper noun** is capitalized and refers to a particular person, place, animal, thing: *Linda, Fluffy, Guelph, Westlane Elementary School*. A **collective noun**, such as *herd, flock, family, community, band, tribe*, is singular when the group is acting as a unit and plural when the group members are acting as individuals.

> The band is on an extended road trip.
> The band are unpacking their instruments.

Object

A word, phrase, or clause that receives the action of the verb or that is governed by a preposition.

> Stephen lent me his pen. [*Me* is the indirect object of the verb *lent*; *pen* is the direct object.]
> She has already left for work. [*Work* is the object of the preposition *for*.]

Parallel Structure

A construction in which ideas of equal importance are expressed in the same grammatical form.

> His analysis is **precise, thorough,** and **perceptive.** [parallel adjectives]
> **What he says** and **what he means** are completely different. [parallel clauses]

Participle

A verb form that can function as a verb or as an adjective. Present participles are formed by adding *ing* to the present tense. Past participles of regular verbs are formed by adding *ed* to the present tense.

When combined with an auxiliary verb, participles become the main verb in a verb phrase (*is laughing, has been dancing, could have finished*).

As adjectives, participles can modify nouns and pronouns (*smiling* face, *running* water, *chipped* tooth, *sworn* testimony; *frowning*, he addressed the assembly).

Part of Speech

Types of words, such as nouns, pronouns, verbs, adjectives, and adverbs.

See *Adjective, Adverb, Conjunction, Interjection, Noun, Preposition, Pronoun, Verb.*

Passive Voice

A construction in which the subject is acted upon by the verb.

> The water was tested for contaminants by the researchers.

In the active voice, this sentence would read:

> The researchers tested the water for contaminants.

Preposition

Prepositions include such words as *by, between, beside, to, of,* and *with.* A preposition, its object (usually a noun or a pronoun), and any words that describe the object make up a prepositional phrase (*towards the deserted beach*). These phrases can function as adjectives (the man *with the red beard*) or as adverbs (walked *down the road,* tired *of waiting*).

Pronoun

A word that substitutes for a noun.

Indefinite Pronouns: *everybody, everyone, everything, somebody, someone, something, nobody, no one, nothing, anybody, anyone, anything, either, neither, each, both, few, several, all*

Personal Subject Pronouns: *I, we, you, he, she, it, they*

Personal Object Pronouns: *me, us, you, him, her, it, them*

Possessive Pronouns: *my, mine, our, ours, you, yours, his, her, hers, its, their, theirs*

Reflexive/Intensive Pronouns: *myself, ourselves, yourself, yourselves, himself, herself, itself, themselves*

Relative Pronouns: *who, whom, which, that, what, whoever, whomever, whichever*

Pronoun Agreement

The principle of matching singular pronouns with singular nouns and pronouns, and plural pronouns with plural nouns and pronouns.

> The **committee** forwarded **its** recommendations.
> **Everyone** has made **his** or **her** views known to the nominating committee.

Pronoun Reference

The principle that every pronoun should clearly refer to a specific noun. See *Antecedent.*

The account that was printed in today's newspaper is completely misleading. [*That* refers to *account*.]

Pronoun Shift

The error of shifting abruptly and with no logical reason from the expected personal pronoun.

I didn't like working in the complaints department because **you** were always dealing with dissatisfied customers.

Split Infinitive

A form of misplaced modifier in which an adverb is placed between *to* and the verb.

to quickly run

Subject

The word or group of words that interact with a verb to establish the basic meaning of a sentence or clause. Subjects are nouns, pronouns, or constructions that function as nouns.

Costs are rising.
To argue with him is a waste of time.
Cleaning the garage is not my idea of a pleasant way to spend the weekend.

Subject-Verb Agreement

The principle of matching singular subjects with singular verbs and plural subjects with plural verbs.

He has his work cut out for him.
They have their work cut out for them.

Subordinate Conjunction

A word used to begin a clause that expresses an idea of subordinate or secondary importance—a subordinate clause. Subordinate conjunctions include words such as *although, because, before, since, while, when, if, until.* See *Clause.*

Subordination

The stylistic technique of expressing less important ideas in subordinate clauses and phrases.

Although I am angry with you, I am still willing to listen to your side of the story.

Tense

The form of the verb that shows its time (past, present, future).

Tense Shift

The error of shifting abruptly and with no obvious reason from one verb tense to another.

Hamlet **was** angry when he **confronts** his mother.

Verb

A word that indicates action (*run, jump, breathe*), sensation (*feel, taste, smell*), possession (*have, own*), existence (*are, were, seem, become*). A verb phrase consists of a main verb (a past or present participle) and one or more auxiliary verbs. For more information on verb phrases, see *Participle* and *Auxiliary Verb*. For more information on verbs, see *Tense, Mood, Active Voice, Passive Voice*, and *Subject-Verb Agreement*.

Keys to Exercises

Part 1: Practice with Writing

Note: Because there are no "right" or "wrong" answers to most of the exercises in Part 1, we are providing only one sample response to the exercises in this section of the book.

Making Reader Profiles - Situation 1

Your response will differ from the one below, depending on the job you are applying for and your own experience and educational background. Just be sure that you are including the same kinds of information.

Sample Response

I've decided to answer a job advertisement for a part-time sales clerk at Eaton's. The advertisement says that positions are available in a number of departments and that additional clerks are needed for evenings and weekends.

1. Who is my reader? The ad says to send applications to the personnel office. I'll phone to get the name of a particular person so that I can address my letter specifically to him or her.
2. What would a person in this position need and want to know? A personnel manager would need to know whether I've had any previous experience in sales, what hours I would be available to work, and which department(s) I would like to work in.
3. What skills and abilities would this reader look for in a prospective employee? To be a good sales clerk a person needs to be familiar with the merchandise and skillful in dealing with the public. Reliability

and enthusiasm for the job will also be significant assets. These are the skills and abilities I'll emphasize.

4. Which aspects of my educational background and work experience should I emphasize? I don't have any previous experience in sales, but I have held other part-time jobs while attending school, so I'll stress my reliability in these positions. I'd like to work in ladies' or children's wear, so I'll emphasize my experience with Eaton's merchandise in these areas. I'll stress my willingness to work on weekends and evenings since part-time employment at these times fits my school schedule.

Part 2: Practice with Sentence Structure, Grammar, and Punctuation

Correcting Sentence Fragments

Exercise 1

1. F
2. S
3. F
4. S
5. F
6. S
7. F
8. F
9. S
10. F

Exercise 2

1. The townspeople waited nervously for the results of the lottery. They knew the winner's fate.

   or

   Knowing the winner's fate, the townspeople waited nervously for the results of the lottery.

2. He has one ambition in life: to travel the world over, seeking fame and fortune.

3. Hoping to hear from you soon, I remain your humble servant.
4. Caroline won the race even though she had a broken bone in her foot.
5. He rushed out the door, raced down the street, and shouted wildly at the bus disappearing in a fog of exhaust fumes.
   or
   Rushing out the door, racing down the street, and shouting wildly at the bus disappearing in a fog of exhaust fumes is not my idea of a good time.

Exercise 3

1. The overcast sky blended with the grey of the land. The horizon appeared to be a confusing smudge of buildings, clouds, haze, and dirty snow. Smoke from metal chimneys drifted aimlessly over the city, mixing with the new flakes that had begun to fall. The streets were a thick stew of decaying snow, salt, and sand, which was churned by the heavy wheels of cars labouring to reach home before an early dusk.
2. Some people regard physical fitness as a means to physical health and well-being. They believe that vigorous exercise strengthens the heart and lengthens life. Other people exercise to make themselves more physically attractive. They want to reshape their bodies to fit the model that society presently holds as representative of physical perfection. Still others are more interested in exercise clothes than in exercise itself. They wear the latest fashions in running shoes, jogging suits, and headbands. But they would never deign to work out for fear that sweat would ruin such expensive gear. Whatever the incentive, people want to be, or want to appear to be, part of the fitness scene. The demand for specialized clothing, equipment, books, video tapes, and memberships in fitness clubs has made exercise a profitable business.

Correcting Comma Faults

Exercise 1

Note: Because there are a number of ways to correct comma faults, each of the sentences below represents only one of several correct versions.

1. She was very nervous during the audition; as a result, her voice cracked several times.
2. The library books were three months overdue; consequently, Marla had to pay a substantial fine.
3. At one o'clock we were still waiting for our friends; finally, we decided to order without them.
4. C

5. The driveway is being framed today. The workers will pour the concrete next week.
6. C
7. Your application was submitted after the deadline; therefore, we cannot consider you for admission this term.
8. Luigi was trying to call Gino at the office; Gino meanwhile was on a plane to Vancouver.
9. "Friends, Romans, countrymen, lend me your ears. I come to bury Caesar, not to praise him."
10. Please lend me the money for a hamburger. I promise to repay you on Tuesday.

Exercise 2

Note: Because sentences containing comma faults can be corrected in a number of different ways, the revised paragraphs below represent only one of a number of possible correct versions.

I planted my garden over the Victoria Day weekend. That was three days ago. Every day I peer intently at the ground, expecting carrots and peas to sprout and grow to maturity before my eyes. So far, there is not so much as a speck of green, and the seeds remain only promises. I have put a great deal of effort into this endeavour, digging, hoeing, raking, planting each seed by hand in beautifully even rows. The vegetables should show some gratitude, at least, for my labours. They might even show a little initiative of their own and make the effort to sprout.

Why are they so reluctant to face life? I promise to take care of them, to water and fertilize them, to cut to the heart any weed and crush to oblivion any insect that threatens their comfort and security. They will not have to fear disease; they will not have to fear devouring slugs. I will help them to grow strong and healthy, to reach vegetable perfection, for that is the least I can do. And when the time comes, they will enjoy a place of honour at my table. That also is the least I can do.

Correcting Fused Sentences

Exercise 1

Note: Because there are a number of ways to correct fused sentences, each of the sentences below represents only one of several possible correct versions.

1. Victoria was queen of Great Britain from 1837 to 1901. After she died, she was succeeded by her son Albert Edward, who became King Edward VII.

2. C
3. The Sphinx challenged every passerby. She demanded to know what walks on four legs in the morning, two in the afternoon, and three in the evening.
4. C
5. Oedipus, returning to Thebes, answered the riddle; the Sphinx then killed herself.
6. Dodos were found on the island of Mauritius in the Indian Ocean. The birds are now extinct.
   or
   Dodos, which were found on the island of Mauritius in the Indian Ocean, are now extinct.
7. Huge flocks of passenger pigeons once filled the skies of North America; however, these birds are now extinct.
8. C
9. The severe thunderstorm has downed the power lines and disrupted service, and so we'll be having cold cuts and salad for supper.
10. By the way, the answer to the Sphinx's riddle is man. He crawls on all fours as a baby, walks upright on two legs in his prime, and uses a cane when he is old.

Exercise 2

Note: The fused sentences in this paragraph can be corrected in several different ways. Note the methods used in the revised paragraph below.

Children now in public school will likely face several career changes in their adult lifetime. Technological developments will make some jobs obsolete, and economic changes will result in decreased demands for certain professions and increased demands for others. It is understandable that a person who has spent several years at a community college, technical institute, or university will want to work in the field for which he or she has been trained. These days, however, fewer members of any graduating class are finding employment in their specific fields. Unemployment becomes a very real prospect. Graduates must therefore be flexible. They must be able to transfer acquired skills to new fields and be willing to learn new skills when needed. Being able to think creatively, read efficiently, and communicate effectively is an integral part of this process.

Correcting Dangling Modifiers

Note: These sentences can be revised in a number of ways. The sentences below present one of several possible correct revisions.

1. When I realized that my airline tickets were still on the coffee table, I asked the taxi driver to turn around and race back to the apartment.
2. After I washed with this beauty soap for seven days, my skin felt soft and smooth.
3. When Walter was a child, model boats were his favourite toys.
4. C
5. Bored by the endless football games on television, I found reading a collection of medieval plays a stimulating change.
6. If you exercise regularly, your strength and endurance will improve.
7. As I waited for the car dealership to open, I looked at several new models.
8. When you are standing out of the sun, the air is chilly.
9. C
10. Because we were exhausted by the steep incline, the top of the hill seemed to be getting farther away.
11. When Lorna was an infant, her parents immigrated to Canada from Scotland.
12. After I had placed the saucer on the floor, the thirsty kitten almost fell into the milk.
13. C
14. After you have smoked one cigarette, carbon dioxide stays in the blood for six hours.
15. After I had phoned her several times to set up an appointment, we finally agreed on a place and time to meet.

Correcting Misplaced Modifiers

1. Recently I read an article in the newspaper about a two-headed calf.
2. Alvin has dug almost the entire garden.
3. The Manchurian elm tree in the front yard was toppled by a severe wind storm.
4. The man disrupting the meeting was ejected from the room.
5. The patient lying on the bed described his out-of-body experience to the doctors.
6. Doctors are now using leeches, for years regarded as loathsome relics of medical quackery, to relieve blood congestion in grafted tissue such as reattached fingers.
   or:
   For years leeches were regarded as loathsome relics of medical quackery, but doctors are now using them to relieve blood congestion in grafted tissue such as reattached fingers.
7. While vacationing on Maui, Mr. and Mrs. Chau saw whales breaching close to shore.

8. John has seen nearly every horror movie made since 1950.
9. C
10. The money representing the net proceeds from the sale of the house was deposited in the bank.
11. In one experiment, a chimpanzee using a portable computer keyboard with special symbols typed a message that he had seen a snake in the woods.
12. C
13. After the fire, Helen was left with only the clothes she was wearing.
14. C
15. After months of intensive research, Rajiv was no closer to knowing how to fit the caramel into the chocolate bar.

Practicing Coordination

1. and
2. but
3. either/or
4. so
5. neither/nor

Correcting Faulty Coordination

1. All three Bronte sisters, Charlotte, Emily, and Anne, were novelists. Charlotte Bronte's best-known work is *Jane Eyre*, published in 1847.
2. Because interest rates have increased in the last month, the Bergmanns are concerned about increased mortgage payments.
   or
   Interest rates have increased in the last month; therefore, the Bergmanns are concerned about increased mortgage payments.
3. When I was reading a magazine, I came across a fascinating article about pet boa constrictors.
4. Beth has good intentions, but sometimes they get her into trouble.
5. At first Marika agreed to write a letter of recommendation for Michael, but when he asked her later, she refused.
6. C
7. Alonzo is a caring and considerate person.
8. When Isaac was sitting under a tree one day, an apple fell and hit him on the head. Suddenly he remembered that he had left an apple pie baking in the oven.
9. C
10. Charles Darwin, a nineteenth-century English naturalist, originated the theory of evolution by natural selection.

Practicing Subordination

Exercise 1

1. Although Alexander loves to skate, he doesn't often get the chance.
2. He spends most of his time working because he has just started his own business.
3. Before he opened a small appliance repair shop, he did some market research on consumer demands.
4. He will be successful if he can solve his problems with part-time employees.
5. He probably won't go skating again until he gets his business under control.

Exercise 2

1. My oldest friend, who lives in Moncton, is coming to spend a month with me this summer.
2. People who plan carefully for retirement experience fewer emotional and financial hardships.
3. My car, which is now ten years old, is starting to have serious mechanical problems.
4. Annalise, who is now in first year university, is living in a big city for the first time.
5. Pets that are bought as Christmas presents are often brought to the SPCA before New Year's Day.

Exercise 3

1. Dr. Hackett, who was our family physician for many years, has recently retired.
   Dr. Hackett, our family physician for many years, has recently retired.
2. Because Larry has just got his driver's licence, he is willing to drive anywhere at any time.
   Having just gotten his driver's licence, Larry is willing to drive anywhere at any time.
3. Alice left the sales meeting feeling quite optimistic because she had made a good presentation.
   Having made a good presentation, Alice left the sales meeting feeling quite optimistic.
4. Cities that are experiencing an economic boom suffer from a shortage of affordable housing.
   Cities experiencing an economic boom suffer from a shortage of affordable housing.

5. Employees who have poor reading and writing skills see no future for themselves with a company.

Employees with poor reading and writing skills see no future for themselves with a company.

Exercise 4

1. Sidney Singh, who just got his papers as a journeyman welder, was among the three workers injured in the oil rig fire.
2. Even though Susan had looked forward to the holiday for months, she found herself reluctant to pack for the trip.
3. C
4. C
5. C
6. After hunting in every closet and drawer in the house, I finally located my birth certificate.
7. This week's TV guide, which I remember leaving on the kitchen table, has disappeared again.
8. C
9. C
10. Unless I hear differently, I'll assume that we'll stick to our original agreement.

Exercise 5

Note: These sentences can be combined in a number of different ways. The answers below present only one possible version.

1. A family in distress may be advised to seek counselling.
2. Most people will have trouble with a therapist who tries to impose his or her own attitudes and morality.
3. If a therapist remains hidden and vague, he or she can expect closed, untrusting behaviour from clients.
4. One very popular approach to family counselling is the systems approach.
5. When children are abused, they learn to see themselves through the eyes of the abuser.
6. Many native children were educated in residential schools because these schools were thought to promote the assimilation of natives into the dominant culture.
7. Many Christian missionaries had no desire to adapt to native cultures because they wanted to change these cultures completely.
8. As long as the traditional Indian way of life remained intact, most Indians saw no reason to adopt a completely different value system, such as Christianity.

9. Because spiritual beliefs permeated every aspect of native cultures, the destruction of these beliefs threatened the whole culture.
10. Indians who converted to Christianity had to reject much of their own culture.

Correcting Faulty Subordination

1. Even though it was pouring rain, Carlos decided to go for his run.
2. In 1951, the Swedish novelist Pär Lagerkvist, who wrote the novel *Barabbas*, won the Nobel Prize for Literature.
3. In 1793, able seaman John Carter of H.M.S. *Discovery*, who was on an expedition to explore part of the British Columbia coast, died from the effects of eating poisonous mussels.
4. Carter was buried in a bay situated about twenty-five kilometres southwest of the cove where the mussels had been found. Captain George Vancouver later named the two locations Poison Cove and Carter Bay.
5. C
6. T. S. Eliot, who once worked as a bank clerk, was a noted poet and literary critic.
7. Because Theo was playing the stereo too loudly, he didn't hear his friend knocking at the door.
8. C
9. Even though the apple tree had an early infestation of tent caterpillars, it produced an excellent crop.
10. Write clear, concise sentences.

Practicing Parallelism

1. his own greed.
2. exploitive
3. looking after it
4. sell it and buy a new one.
5. shelter.
6. make important decisions.
7. the best interests of the family.
8. well paying.
9. sent to live with strangers.
10. fallen asleep.

Correcting Faulty Parallelism

Exercise 1

1. and that I would like her to call me tonight.
2. Not only did she return the car with an empty tank but she also dented the back fender.
3. Either Stephen will visit his parents in Ontario
4. but less dependable than Henry.
5. and leave the key under the mat.

Exercise 2

1. and howling cats.
2. because of heavy accumulations of snow and ice.
3. to renting an apartment.
4. but that she doesn't have enough money this week.
5. both practical and decorative.
6. C
7. an egg sandwich, a glass of milk, and a piece of pumpkin pie.
8. by climbing over the fence and crossing the field.
9. C
10. but of ordinary men.
11. and because he has excellent references from previous employers.
12. and planting a few trees.
13. and the left headlight is chipped.
14. C
15. nutritious meals for the children. Every worker has

Correcting Mixed Constructions

1. Although he knew that smoking was harmful, he continued to smoke two packs a day.
   or
   He knew that smoking was harmful; however, he continued to smoke two packs a day.
2. Without confirmed hotel reservations and a return ticket, a traveller won't get past immigration officials at the island's international airport.
3. Because the driveway hasn't been poured yet, we have to park on the street.
4. To put something over on people is to trick or deceive them.
5. This movie appeals to both critics and the general public.
6. I don't know how much it will cost to repair the furnace.

7. One reason why this child has trouble learning is that she doesn't get enough to eat.
8. Paula reached the front door of the Smiths' house before she realized that the party was the following Saturday.
9. I'll let you decide whether to order pizza or Chinese food.
10. Lynne was more interested in reading a novel than in watching reruns of *Gilligan's Island*.
11. To put up with something you don't like means you tolerate it.
12. The photograph taken by the undercover police officer shows the accused accepting a package from a known mobster.
13. The more books I read, the less I seem to remember.
14. Fortunately, he's the type of student who both knows and cares about his work.
15. Jimmy is cranky because he's tired today.
16. The enclosed directions explain how to put the model together.
17. Learning to skate as a child is easier than learning to skate as an adult.
18. Because their son's baseball tournament is this weekend, the Malaks won't be going to the lake.
   or
   Their son's baseball tournament is this weekend; therefore, the Malaks won't be going to the lake.
19. I should either revise this essay completely or start over again with a different topic.
20. Dermabelle Products is sending out questionnaires asking consumers how they rate the company's soap.

Recognizing Auxiliary Verbs

1. (has) written

2. (should have) heard

3. (is used to) eating

4. (will be) going

5. (did) submit

6. (has been) visiting

7. (would be) going

8. (might have) gotten

9. (have to) cook

10. (must have been) stolen

Common Problems with Auxiliaries

Exercise 1

1. *Skiing* is a noun. *Used to be* is the verb.
2. *Skating* is an adjective describing *party*. *Ought to hold* is the verb.
3. *Is being* is the verb.
4. *Painting* and *sculpting* are adjectives describing classes.
   Will be held is the verb.
5. *Will be cleaning* is the verb.

Exercise 2

1. new car is
2. Chris runs
3. friends are waiting / were waiting / waited
4. shoes in the store cost
5. that amount is

Exercise 3

1. Sidney has gone
2. Allison has become
3. The baby hasn't drunk
4. he immediately rang the fire alarm.
5. Mrs. Kishimoto has driven
6. the young child had broken
7. had shrunk
8. Have you chosen a topic
9. We saw Wayne Gretzky
10. I have torn a hole

Exercise 4

1. I might have guessed
2. If I had phoned the airport
3. Peter would have written if he had had your address.
4. Paulette ought to have finished
5. C

Exercise 5

1. If we had arrived

2. haven't spoken
3. socks are
4. shouldn't have sat
5. He has come
6. fans were rushing / fans rushed
7. couldn't have gone
8. C
9. if I had known
10. he has run

Correcting Errors with Irregular Verbs

Exercise 1

1. was, been
2. beat, beaten
3. bore, borne
4. became, become
5. began, begun
6. bound, bound
7. bought, bought
8. burst, burst
9. caught, caught
10. chose, chosen
11. clung, clung
12. came, come
13. cost, cost
14. dived/dove, dived
15. did, done
16. dreamed/dreamt, dreamed/dreamt
17. drank, drunk
18. ate, eaten
19. fell, fallen
20. flew, flown
21. forgave, forgiven
22. froze, frozen
23. got, got/gotten
24. went, gone
25. ground, ground
26. hit, hit
27. held, held
28. kept, kept

29. kneeled/knelt, kneeled/knelt
30. laid, laid
31. led, led
32. left, left
33. lay, lain
34. lost, lost
35. proved, proved/proven
36. read, read
37. rode, ridden
38. rose, risen
39. saw, seen
40. set, set
41. shook, shaken
42. shot, shot
43. showed, showed/shown
44. sang, sung
45. spoke, spoken
46. stood, stood
47. swam, swum
48. took, taken
49. taught, taught
50. thought, thought

Exercise 2

1. have been fighting / have fought
2. left, worn
3. bitten
4. sung / been singing
5. come
6. saw
7. left
8. known
9. slept / been sleeping
10. swum
11. run
12. drunk
13. gone
14. hidden
15. is

Exercise 3

1. He has led
2. Paul is used to having
3. were hung upside down.
4. I chose
5. if she lies in the sun much longer.
6. C
7. By the time Marcus had lain down
8. All applications must reach
9. When you lose work done on a computer
10. C

Exercise 4

1. The car was supposed
2. Have you swum
3. C
4. that he drank
5. Marlene loses
6. as the trainer led
7. lie down
8. C
9. Witnesses saw
10. We used to order

Using Prepositions with Verbs

Exercise 1

1. differs from
2. bored with
3. agree to
4. agree with
5. compare with

Exercise 2

1. differ from
2. warned against
3. participates in
4. succeeded in

5. depends on/upon
6. abstain from
7. compared to
8. count on
9. dispense with
10. immunized against

The Passive Voice

Exercise 1

1. P
2. A
3. A
4. P
5. P
6. A
7. P
8. P
9. P
10. A

Exercise 2

1. The fire was started by children playing with matches.
2. The alarm was sounded by three people who saw smoke and flames coming from a ground floor window.
3. The children were rescued by a police officer who happened upon the scene.
4. Maxine was bitten by a dog.
5. The petition was signed by over five hundred people.

Correcting Errors in Subject-Verb Agreement

Exercise 1

1. looks very appetizing
2. has been taken
3. C
4. *The Wars* . . . was made
5. The number of unemployed people grows

6. The volunteer group is collecting
7. Ninety thousand dollars is too much
8. Measles is spreading rapidly
9. Bread and butter is delicious by itself
10. C

Exercise 2

1. are
2. has
3. are
4. tastes
5. are
6. is
7. is
8. is
9. has been
10. have

Exercise 3

1. who have been assassinated
2. Gandhi . . . was
3. his fight . . . was
4. the number . . . was
5. were two methods
6. neither . . . was
7. C
8. attempts . . . were
9. somebody . . . was
10. neither Gandhi nor Martin Luther King has

Correcting Errors In Pronoun Agreement

Exercise 1

1. has made his [her] position
2. They can, however, be overcome.
3. C
4. have lost their original brightness.
5. expressed her satisfaction.

Exercise 2

1. wants to have his or her name
2. C
3. C
4. feels that his or her job
5. C
6. If anyone submits his or her paper early
7. No one is allowed to leave his or her seat
8. C
9. has reached its destination.
10. Someone or something put its bony fingers

Exercise 3

1. Single parents need more flexibility in arranging their class timetables.
   or
   The single parent needs more flexibility in arranging his or her class timetable.
2. Effective administrators maintain good relations with all their staff members.
   or
   An effective administrator maintains good relations with all his or her staff members.
3. Floundering first-year students need to be encouraged to contact their instructors for extra help.
   or
   The floundering first-year student needs to be encouraged to contact his or her instructor for extra help.
4. C
5. Depressed teenagers are often unwilling to reveal their problems to their parents or teachers.

Exercise 4

1. The team has just finished its seventh
2. The dinner theatre audience ordered their drinks
3. C
4. The dance committee presented its proposals
5. The stolen property has been returned to its owner.

Exercise 5

1. will give us his expert advice
2. C
3. Neither the doctor nor the patients felt that their needs
4. will present her views
5. will drive his car

Exercise 6

1. <u>Anyone</u> who wins a lottery must allow his or her name
2. A <u>person</u> who thinks . . . his or her mind.
   or
   <u>People</u> who think . . . their minds.
3. Every <u>customer</u> who purchases . . . his or her name
   or
   <u>Customers</u> who purchase . . . their names
4. C [<u>Course</u> is the antecedent of *which*.]
5. The <u>dog</u> that is wandering . . . its way home.
6. C [*People* is the antecedent of *who*.]
7. A <u>child</u> who feels that his or her needs
8. Marvin is the <u>person</u> . . . who washes his car
9. A single <u>woman</u> who lives . . . her drapes drawn.
10. C [*People* is the antecedent of *who*.]

Exercise 7

1. Only themselves
2. C
3. cut himself or herself
4. The restaurant manager himself
5. for us and for themselves.

Exercise 8

1. has its legends
2. about them.
3. around his neck
4. his or her portion
5. his or her own idea
6. they must have been made
7. he abandons her there.
8. C

9. makes its appearance
10. among his or her ancestors.

Correcting Errors in Pronoun Case

Exercise 1

1. We nonsmokers
2. as she.
3. Marilyn and he
4. his wife and he
5. they who are
6. C
7. her grandmother and she
8. He and I
9. Michael, Joey, and I
10. older than she.

Exercise 2

1. on Howard and him.
2. to Philip and me.
3. with whom I share it.
4. my friends and me.
5. Marco or him
6. C
7. Andreas and her
8. C
9. between you and me.
10. my parents and me.

Exercise 3

1. its
2. Who's
3. It's
4. whose
5. its
6. Whose
7. It's
8. Who's
9. its

10. who's

Exercise 4

1. It's
2. C
3. Everyone's
4. its
5. whose
6. C
7. One's, one's
8. C
9. whose
10. C

Exercise 5

1. Martha and she
2. its usual place.
3. C
4. from Bertha or me
5. faster than he.
6. George and I
7. Christine and I
8. C
9. Kevin and her
10. C
11. sent to her
12. its den.
13. Someone's
14. C
15. we business students

Correcting Errors in Pronoun Reference

1. Karl told Edward, "You [or I] will run the company one day."
2. Trudy ran in the race even though she had a bad cold and a strained muscle.
3. Although Mr. Lincoln regarded himself as an intelligent and flexible person, the personnel office [or the employment counsellor] told him that he was too old to begin a new career.
4. The company must lay off fifty employees because costs have increased and profits have declined.

271

5. When Peter contacted the telephone company, the receptionist said the company would send a repair person the next day.
6. I used to have trouble sticking with my decision not to drink, but now that I'm attending AA meetings regularly not drinking is much easier.
7. Not many people are attracted to a job in a bush camp because it involves long hours, demanding working conditions, and long stretches of isolation.
8. Twenty train cars were derailed, but no one was injured in the accident.
9. The computer literacy course is extremely useful, but Maria was discouraged because it is hard to get into.
10. When the doctor phoned the cardiac ICU to check for space, the staff said that nothing was available.

Maintaining a Consistent Point of View: Avoiding Pronoun Shifts

Note: This paragraph could be revised a number of ways. Because the intention seems to be to give advice, *you* is a good pronoun to use as it establishes the closest relationship between the writer and the reader. You could revise this paragraph, however, by referring to *homebuyers* and *their* needs throughout. This is what the paragraph looks like when *you* is used.

Planning to buy a new home involves a number of important decisions. You can choose from a variety of housing types, including single family dwellings and multiple family dwellings, such as duplexes and townhomes. You must consider such requirements as proximity to work, schools, and shopping; the number of bathrooms and bedrooms; and the size of the yard. You must also consider whether to purchase an existing home or have one built for you. Many of your decisions will depend on personal lifestyle and preferences, but they will depend even more on your financial resources. It may be sobering for you to realize that what you want in a home and what you can afford can be very far apart indeed.

Practice with Troublesome Adjectives and Adverbs

Exercise 1

1. quietly
2. worst
3. well
4. less happy
5. badly

6. most beautiful
7. really good.
8. more determined.
9. can hardly
10. fewer

Exercise 2

1. charitable donations
2. those flowers
3. C
4. administrative costs
5. as if

Practice with Commas

Exercise 1

1. invitations, and Sharon
2. merchandise, shop
3. The rest, it seems to me, is up to you.
4. yet, although
5. the trip, for they
6. C
7. answers, nor could
8. ate, the adults.
9. "That sounds delicious," my companion replied,
10. C
11. library stacks, but someone
12. As we stood watching, the building
13. C
14. Stella, who is organizing the dance, has scheduled
15. Magnetic Hill, which is located near Moncton, is an optical illusion.
16. C
17. The mouse ran up the clock, the clock struck one, and the mouse ran down.
18. The problem, I realized, was
19. C
20. C

Exercise 2

1. Renaissance, the great revival of learning that marked

2. mukluks, Murray felt
3. No, Clarence hasn't
4. However, I'll have him call you
5. requires bedding, shoes, clothing, and canned goods.
6. Australia, not South America
7. Above, the stars looked like diamonds.
8. baby, Mrs. Bigelow
9. C
10. Chantilly, a delicate lace, is named
11. The family moved to Fergus, Ontario, on July 1, 1967.
12. We hope, Mr. Ventura, that you
13. The Sartorial Emporium, now closed for renovations, will
14. Sir Frederick Banting, the co-discoverer of insulin,
15. Wapiti, for example,
16. the complex, intricate puzzle.
17. C
18. The cheque, as a matter of fact, is in the mail.
19. two metres high, you must
20. C

Exercise 3

1. abruptly, Wendy
2. Witches, ghosts, and goblins . . . Halloween, which
3. tickets, we were faced
4. However, we decided
5. interview, he was unshaven and unkempt, and he complained
6. subsided, the community
7. in time, but
8. cake, and [or no comma]
9. Cook Islands, not the
10. paint the fence, repair the leaky faucet, and plant
11. homonyms, words that have
12. soft, creamy
13. C
14. effect, many scientists agree,
15. C
16. Eve, isn't it?
17. Judith, carrying two heavy suitcases, rushed
18. tired, hungry, and thirsty
19. April 14, 1912, on her
20. Toronto, Ontario.

Practice With Semicolons

1. two more years; then
2. mirrors life; it can
3. and beef; Greek salad with tomatoes, onions, and feta cheese; and chocolate cake
4. the subject; however, Joseph
5. a tooth filled; I'm therefore always happy
6. between flights; otherwise, we might
7. subflooring; then they
8. were effective; but the judges
9. to an end; others
10. the course; consequently,

Practice with Colons and Dashes

1. to the next class: a dictionary,
2. the merger—the president, two vice-presidents, and the sales manager—will
3. the matter—we had expected he might—and
4. provocation: [or—] the victim said
5. traditional love sonnets: "My mistress'
6. Thursday at 8:15 a.m.
7. employees: a free
8. mesmerized: they were awed
9. This picture—isn't it beautiful?—was painted
10. only two things: [or—] a double cheeseburger

Practice with Apostrophes

Exercise 1

1. contraction
2. possessive
3. plural
4. possessive
5. possessive

Exercise 2

1. 1930s (1930's)

2. Lindas
3. SPCA's
4. *therefore*'s
5. *a*'s

Exercise 3

1. the stewardesses' wages
2. the Jacksons' new car
3. Mark and Lenore's bank account
4. cattle's hooves
5. this pair of scissors' blades
6. Tina's and George's cars
7. the bee's knees
8. Charles's trumpet
9. sister-in-law's apartment
10. friendship's reward

Exercise 4

1. no apostrophes
2. no apostrophes
3. It's
4. '86.
5. 80's ['80s]
6. Who's
7. I'd/I'll
8. no apostrophes
9. It's
10. She'd/who's

Exercise 5

1. linked *l*'s
2. the Martins' house
3. We've/I'm/it's
4. Brenda's mother-in-law's/this year's
5. players'
6. no apostrophes [or 1980's]
7. parents'/they're
8. Someone's
9. *hopefully*'s
10. men's/children's

Practice with Italics and Quotation Marks

Exercise 1

1. *modus operandi*
2. *Enterprise / Star Trek: The Next Generation*
3. *An Enemy of the People*
4. *cum grano salis* ["with a grain of salt"; not too seriously]
5. *Queen of Saanich*

Exercise 2

1. "Where am I?" asked Cynthia. "Is this a hospital?"
2. "I'm afraid I planted too much zucchini this year," remarked my neighbour, handing me a dozen gigantic squash.
3. Do you think Mrs. Macomber deliberately shot her husband in Hemingway's story "The Short Happy Life of Francis Macomber"?
4. *Chez moi* means "at my house."
5. Who wrote the poem that begins "Shall I compare thee to a summer's day?"

Exercise 3

1. James Thurber's story "The Secret Life of Walter Mitty" first appeared in *The New Yorker* in 1939.
2. "I can never," asserted Lady Ashley, "forgive such barbarous cruelty."
3. The Greek expression *eureka* means "I have found it!"
4. The theme of *carpe diem* ("seize the day") reaches its most vivid expression in Andrew Marvell's poem "To His Coy Mistress" in the lines "The grave's a fine and private place / But none, I think, do there embrace."
5. Is the U2 song "Angel of Harlem" on *The Joshua Tree* or *Rattle and Hum*?
6. In the chapter titled "The Early Life of the Morels," D. H. Lawrence sets out the reasons for the conflict between Mr. and Mrs. Morel, a conflict that pervades the whole of his early novel, *Sons and Lovers*.
7. Her favourite Beatles' song is "Yesterday."
8. He claims to be an "enlightened despot." He is half right, at least.
9. "Do you understand my point?" Mitch asked, jabbing his pencil into my arm.
10. The motto of the French Revolution was *"Liberté, Egalité, Fraternité"* ("Liberty, Equality, Brotherhood").

Practice with Parentheses and Brackets

1. (I must confess) **or** (impatiently, I must confess)
2. "Prooffread [*sic*]
3. (each plane to the left of the one in front of it).
4. (1882-1945)
5. (a) the cost, (b) the personnel, (c) the amount of time

Practice with End Punctuation

Exercise 1

1. hockey player.
2. pies? jam? jelly?
3. lives!
4. Red Death"?
5. C

Exercise 2

1. science.
2. light?
3. immediately!
4. restaurant.
5. can I?
6. dinner?"
7. Help!/car!
8. NATO?
9. ninety?/bus.
10. fettle"?

Practice with Abbreviations

1. assistant, Dr.
2. Reverend O'Connor
3. Christmas/Alberta.
4. A.D. 26-36
5. Professor Whiteley/ 6:30 p.m.
6. Mrs. C. D. Laing, Jr.
7. Dr. James Lee **or** James Lee, M.D.
8. 469-399 B.C.
9. August.
10. kilometres

11. Roger McKerracher, Ph.D./ professor/ history department.
12. Eileen and Carol / physical education.
13. Winnipeg, Manitoba
14. River Road
15. UNESCO.
16. Mr. and Mrs. Chimko / anniversary.
17. United States.
18. *Laser*, *maser*, and *radar* are some of the acronyms now considered common nouns.
19. September 28 / 3.6 kilograms.
20. TNT / used, for example,

Practice with Capitalization

1. history / *Bounty* / Captain / South
2. Mother / Aunt / Christmas.
3. high school / Victorian
4. Brock's Monument / Queenston Heights.
5. French
6. Do
7. that
8. northernmost / Bear / Polaris / North
9. *Streetcar Named Desire* / Marlon Brando
10. doctor's / high blood pressure.
11. Sociology 200 / English 210 / fall
12. Uncle / like
13. World War II / Europe / forces
14. north / south
15. Latin

Practice with Hyphens

Exercise 1

1. cal-endar **or** calen-dar
2. diet-ary
3. fill-ing
4. hero-ism
5. dropped
6. UNICEF
7. C
8. C
9. never-theless
10. medium

Exercise 2

1. father-in-law
2. self-indulgent
3. anti-American
4. lily of the valley
5. lily-livered
6. ex-stock broker
7. quickly scribbled note
8. two-thirds empty
9. mouthwash
10. ground zero
11. landed immigrant
12. great-aunt
13. eighty-seven
14. eel-like aquatic vertebrate
15. fusion bomb
16. well-written paper
17. mayor-elect
18. keepsake
19. outfielder
20. blackboard

Exercise 3

1. part-time
2. holier-than-thou
3. pre-election
4. nineteenth- and twentieth-century
5. left-handed
6. honky-tonk
7. devil-may-care
8. twenty-three
9. small-minded / ill-tempered
10. all-clear

Practice Using Numbers

1. eight o'clock
2. Fifteen dollars
3. C
4. ten thousand needy families
5. 5 percent
6. C
7. ten million dollars / September 30, 1989.
8. Twelve hundred
9. $10.95
10. C

Part 3: How Words Work

Basic Spelling Rules

Exercise 1

1. companies
2. handkerchiefs
3. women
4. babies
5. thieves
6. cupfuls
7. halves
8. criteria
9. heroes
10. sisters-in-law

Exercise 2

The fifteen misspelled words in this paragraph are: argument, difficulties, said, sufficient, running, dictionaries, mysterious, height, noticeably, their, easily, preferred, continuous, piece, writing.

Using a Dictionary

Exercise 1: Spelling

1. C
2. athlete
3. occurrence
4. inconvenient
5. privilege
6. definitely
7. develop
8. C
9. tragedy
10. fundamental

Exercise 2: Syllabication

1. heav • en • ly
2. im • ple • ment
3. kind•li•ness
4. di • no • saur
5. mod • i • fy
6. a • maze • ment
7. al • to • geth • er
8. oc • cur • rence
9. pin • a • fore
10. re • un • ion

Exercise 3: Pronunciation

1. rely
2. inventory
3. alienation
4. masterful
5. conscientious
6. ornamental
7. uniform
8. reverse
9. partially
10. hospital

Exercise 4: Parts of Speech

1. noun
2. verb (transitive)
3. interjection
4. conjunction
5. adverb
6. adjective
7. verb (transitive)
8. verb (intransive)
9. adjective
10. noun

Exercise 5: Etymology

1. Dutch
2. Italian
3. Latin

4. Chinook
5. Chinese

Exercise 6: Meanings

1. lie: a) to recline (lie on a bed)
        b) to misrepresent the truth (tell a lie)
2. cone: a) a geometric shape (a dunce cap is cone-shaped)
        b) the fruit of a pine or fir tree (a pine cone)
3. drop: a) a small quantity of liquid (a tear drop)
        b) to decrease in value (a drop in prices)
4. game: a) an amusement (a game of darts)
        b) wildlife shot for sport (wild game hunting)
5. foot: a) a unit of measurement (one foot long)
        b) the part of the leg used for standing (to stand on one foot)

INDEX

Boldface terms are included in the Glossary of Grammatical Terms (241-249).